Living For Tomorrow

I0809532

Living For Tomorrow

How to Survive Any Catastrophe

By

Brent Lee, PhD

CFI
Springville, Utah

© 2009 Brent Lee

All rights reserved.

No part of this book may be reproduced in any form whatsoever, whether by graphic, visual, electronic, film, microfilm, tape recording, or any other means, without prior written permission of the publisher, except in the case of brief passages embodied in critical reviews and articles.

This is not an official publication of The Church of Jesus Christ of Latter-day Saints. The opinions and views expressed herein belong solely to the author and do not necessarily represent the opinions or views of Cedar Fort, Inc. Permission for the use of sources, graphics, and photos is also solely the responsibility of the author.

The views expressed within this work are the sole responsibility of the author and do not necessarily reflect the position of Cedar Fort, Inc., or any other entity.

ISBN 13: 978-1-59955-223-1

Published by CFI, an imprint of Cedar Fort, Inc., 2373 W. 700 S., Springville, UT 84663
Distributed by Cedar Fort, Inc., www.cedarfort.com

Library of Congress Cataloging-in-Publication Data

Lee, Brent.
Living for tomorrow : how to survive any catastrophe / Brent Lee.
p. cm.
ISBN 978-1-59955-223-1
1. Survival skills. 2. Disasters. I. Title.

GF86.L44 2008
613.6'9--dc22

2008041849

Cover design by Angela Olsen
Cover design © 2009 by Lyle Mortimer
Edited and typeset by Natalie A. Hepworth

Printed in the United States of America

10 9 8 7 6 5 4 3 2 1

Printed on acid-free paper

To my wife,
Fe Lee,
and my kids,
Brian, Eric, Nicol, and Chris

Also By Brent Lee

Beyond Knowing
Epicenter

Contents

Acknowledgments

The successful completion of this book was, and is, a team effort. I want to thank each of you for your contribution, because your moment of sharing was very important to me.

I want to thank my son Chris for his questions, and for his inspiration to never give up—to keep going forward despite the conflicts that pop up in front of me. In a way, this book was written to help him and the rest of my children find their way home.

I would also like to thank George Edward Mills IV for his ideas and concepts. And his patience when reading the various rough versions of this manuscript as it slowly transformed into what it is today.

I owe a tremendous debt to Lorne "Joe" Doty for reminding me of the hardships we experienced in the mid-1970s, when the destructive powers of Super Typhoon Pamela struck Guam, and of the two major earthquakes that followed. And for the complexity of questions he asked that kept me digging for more information.

I would also like to extend a very special thanks to Dan Crooked Arm, EMS, of the Turtle Mountain Chippewa for various concepts concerning water purification, medical wellness, and the importance of ensuring our families have current vaccinations.

And last but not least, I want to thank Tony Crow Eagle of the Turtle Mountain Chippewa for sharing his lifetime of experience. Thank you for letting me see how easy it is to achieve harmony with nature.

Again, from the bottom of my heart, I want to thank all the people who helped make this book possible.

Foreword

By George Edward Mills IV

Survival Planner

This marvelous informational and strategic planning handbook is a completely useful manual for self-preservation. During the troubled times to come, many people will suffer needless heartache and die from consequences beyond their ability to cope with complex situations. Simple planning and daily thought may protect you and your family from disaster. Do not allow your family to be lost simply because you did not plan. Many people fear being branded as either a doomsayer or a radical, when all they really desire is to be prepared for events in a future scenario steeped in uncontrollable possibilities.

As all good Boy Scouts know, being prepared can mean the difference between comfortable survival and meaningless suffering. The facts and suggestions you are about to read may prove invaluable to the people who may repopulate our earth. Simple steps such as primitive camping practice and survival preparation will make all the difference. This does not sound so radical to me, and I hope it allows you to think about survival as a step toward regaining normality in a world gone crazy with strife and grief. After all, do we not currently plan for our families, for spending, and for retirement? Therefore, is it so drastic for anyone to plan for a future that will contain great uncertainty? I feel this survival-planning manual will help you and your family enjoy life and promote positive thoughts about an uncertain future. Please read the following suggestions and contemplate your responses, study all possible avenues, and research every aspect of the information enclosed—for your very life may depend upon your reaction.

Introduction

If disaster of the worst kind struck, would you be prepared? What would you do if the sky were literally falling? Where would you go to seek safety from a solar storm? Would your present geographical location be safe? How would you deal with volcanic ash, mud rain, and the pitch-black of a moonless night in the middle of the day? Or smoke so thick from a major fire that it would physically hurt your lungs and eyes if you went outside? Would you be able to deal with the social and economic downfall during the aftermath?

What would you do if you were confronted by terrorists, highway bandits, marauders, or people just trying to stay alive? Would you be able to keep it together and save your family? And what about the elderly, sick family members, or your pets or livestock? Do you have a plan in place or know where to find such a plan that would help you lead your loved ones to a safe haven?

What could possibly happen that would be so devastating that we would need a survival plan?

Each night the National Weather Service shows us computer projections from the National Oceanic and Atmosphere Administration (NOAA) to help us prepare for tomorrow's weather. In addition, the Discovery Channel and the National Geographic Channel have presented various shows based on combined reports from the NOAA, the U.S. Geological Survey (USGS), and the National Aeronautics and Space Administration (NASA) to show us the possibilities of the near future. These programs concerning super storms, volcanoes, asteroids, solar storms, changing weather patterns, global warming, and so forth, are not a work of fiction, but computer simulations of possible future events based on the facts being studied today. And when we add the research of ancient documents to the computer simulation, we now have a detrimental futuristic model of global proportions that will affect the complete human race. An example of one large asteroid body discussed in ancient documents is the projected return of Nibiru in 2012. If you are not familiar with who or what Nibiru is, it is a well-documented spatial object that passes through our galaxy every three thousand years—and it's on its way back.

What do we do? We educate ourselves. We familiarize ourselves with the numerous response plans being used by the various governments of Earth and large corporations. We also look to numerous international organizations that use up-to-date computer data from the NOAA and its counterparts, the USGS and their counterparts, NASA, the World Bank's projections on the economic reaction and downfall, and the compiled research of ancient documents concerning the return of previous asteroids and planets.

Or you can read this book.

Either way, we will discover a common thread of concern in all the agencies' reports that contradict the news releases to the public: Earth's climate is changing at an exponential pace and will affect all aspects of society. We will ascertain a personal understanding of the pandemic fear of the future of life on Earth that our government has kept from us.

But it does not stop there. Our government, along with all the other governments of our world, and international corporations have survival manuals that come in volumes—not chapters. Our government's survival manuals were created to protect and ensure our elected officials' survival so they can pick up the pieces. They were not designed to protect you and me. We are on our own.

What is the next step? Would it behoove us to be prepared and never have to use our survival plan, rather than be unprepared and face the possible loss of loved ones because we chose to wait and see? Once the worst happens, our plan (or lack of it) will be our only guide as we deal with Earth's greatest pains that will fall upon us with no consideration for wealth, education, race, or religion. It will come equally to all of us, for Mother Nature will show no mercy when she unleashes her wrath, whether it be caused by mankind's pollution or nuclear weapons, or her reaction to solar storms, asteroids, or the atrocities of a gravitational battle between the Sun and Nibiru, and we will be passengers along for an inescapable ride.

When do we need to start? Yesterday would have been best, but today will do. We have a basic understanding of what lies ahead, and this book will help you prepare a plan today so that you and your family will survive the events of tomorrow.

And for those of you who already sense an approaching danger, are dreaming of disaster, or feel that time is of the essence, this book is reassuring for each of you. It will lead you step-by-step through a practical process so you can prepare to survive. Regardless of whether you can afford to build a bunker or barely afford to buy a shovel, the information in this book is designed to be equally useful. The process is simple, and this book will show you how easy it is for you to prepare. The sooner you begin, the better your odds of survival will be.

The Reality of Life

We are safe! That's what I want to believe, don't you? And when we feel insecure, we have the right to financially purchase an item or hire a service that gives us back our personal comfort zone of safety. Unfortunately, this belief hinges on our trust in the economy and the support of the vast majority of the human race living in industrialized nations that rely upon a materialistic consumer existence. In today's environment, this consumer survival reaction serves us well, but in the times to come, it lacks the breadth and flexibility to be a true survival paragon—it holds no clues or path to follow for survival.

How We See the World

An old adage tells us, "What doesn't kill you makes you stronger." The logic is sound, but will it be enough? For decades, governments and powerful corporations have been preparing for various cataclysms on a scale that few may imagine. Or have we? How many of you have watched sci-fi movies about killer tornadoes, super storms, asteroids, earthquakes, volcanic eruptions, solar storms, or nuclear war? Were those movies based on truth? Yes. And did we want to see that truth? No, because our lives are already full of problems: both parents work and the husband has recently started a second job. We also deal with a variable rate mortgage, credit cards, cell phones, the ever-increasing food prices, gasoline, and utilities—then there are all the things the kids need. If disaster did strike, it could actually bring relief because all our present-day problems would go away. And then our present problems could be replaced with an unimaginable nightmare. To illustrate the point, let's see how Joe decides to respond:

Joe would be the perfect "poster boy" for middle-class America. He lives in the suburbs on an average middle-class income. He is married to his college sweetheart and they have two children, a dog, a cat, and two economy-class automobiles in the garage. One day at work, Joe overhears a group of coworkers talking about the possible destruction of the human race by an approaching asteroid. At first, Joe dismisses it—until he sees his boss involved in the conversation. Joe's curiosity and concern for his future are piqued. That evening, he seeks out and reads several articles about asteroid strikes and how they could also trigger volcanoes and cause destructive super storms. After sharing his discovery with his wife, Joe decides to use a survival plan downsized from a government disaster proposal. The first thing Joe does is build a six-foot fence around his back yard to block prying eyes.

To add additional security to his secret survival plan, Joe decides to work at night, and he plays music with a boom box to drown out the construction of a nice bunker under a beautiful gazebo. When it is finished, Joe stocks it full of supplies: food, fuel, weapons, and ammunition to last at least a year. After the bunker is sealed, Joe hugs his wife and, with a secure inner feeling, he heads down to the bank and refinances the house so they can buy a brand new 4x4. Now they are set. They get on with their lives, confident that they have the best secret survival plan in the neighborhood.

As luck goes, disaster strikes while Joe and the family are out of town visiting relatives. Joe explains to the relatives that it would be safer to return home than remain there. Total chaos ensues, and Joe leaves the safety of relatives behind. Power lines are down, the Red Cross is running out of supplies, and the National Guard is patrolling the roads and byways. The stores are out of everything. Joe smiles reassuringly to his wife and kids, and again explains how lucky they are; the 4x4 is full of gas, and they have just enough fuel to make it home to their bunker. Joe smiles to himself, feeling safe and secure with the survival plan.

The going is rough because bridges have collapsed, super tornadoes have destroyed huge parts of the countryside, and dams have given-way, releasing tyrants of destruction that show no mercy for whatever lies before them. None of that seems to bother Joe, for those conditions are where a 4x4 shines. He again pats himself on the back. What a great foresight on his part!

After clearing the final checkpoint and the thorough inspection for weapons, the 4x4 starts to cough. Starved for fuel, it barely gets them into the driveway before the engine fails. That's okay—Joe reminds everyone that they have 100 gallons of fuel in the bunker. Again, Joe feels secure as they jump out of the 4x4 and run around to their backyard. No worries.

The next thing Joe knows, he is standing there looking at the pile of debris that was once the gazebo and what's left of the bunker—everything is gone. As the reality of it sinks in, Joe's wife nudges him in the ribs and motions for Joe to look up.

There, looking down at them from atop the 6-foot fence are their neighbors. They are aiming Joe's guns at him, loaded with his ammunition, and they've only got one question: Where's the other bunker?

If that does not disturb you, then here's another situation. Let us look at the people who do not pay any attention to life around them until fate falls upon them. This example is about the urban survivalist who waits until the last minute to go shopping.

Bill's first surprise was finding hoards of people at the grocery store trying to do the same thing. What had started out as a fine day came crashing down around him as Bill's mood reflected his frustration of having to park so far from the grocery store. Bill is surprised by the commotion in the parking lot, and initially thinks how stupid some people are acting, as he walks around two people fist-fighting over the contents of a spilled grocery cart. After shoving and pushing to gain entrance, he stands in shock at the realization that the canned goods he wants are gone—and he doesn't want to survive on canned lima beans or sauerkraut. Bill fights his way out of that aisle. After being pushed, shoved around, and bruised from being knocked down by an angry, foul-mouthed woman pushing an over-stocked shopping cart, he finds himself delightfully surprised by the gold mine of food before him. Bill hurries to gather as much as the cart will hold and fights his way through the crowds, eventually arriving at the checkout counter.

Finally safe at home, Bill walks in, beaming proudly at his accomplishments, and proclaims to his family that he has saved the day. But wondering if all of it will fit in the freezer, Bill surveys the bags doubtfully. "I don't know. We may have to eat the frozen food stuff for a couple of days." After everything was snugly packed away, we leave this survivor thinking he's prepared; and the thought of the electricity going out never crosses his mind.

Why did this happen to these people? They reacted like a consumer—not like a survivor. Consumers dig bunkers, fill them with supplies, and buy practical survival vehicles like 4x4's. Or they wait until the last minute and purchase useless supplies. Then, they feel free to resume their usual routine, knowing in the back of their minds they have a plan. Survivors on the other hand prepare in a very different way.

Why Does a Survivor Plan Ahead?

A survivor seeks the information needed to prepare. A survivor knows that all the time in the world will not help if we do not have any idea why we need a survival plan. Therefore a question arises: What is going to happen that will be so devastating that we will need a survival plan?

Our government has departments full of researchers who study all possible aspects and have used that time to prepare numerous governmental survival plans. They have seen all the computer scenarios concerning the explosive pace of Earth's changing weather and its effect on the global economy. Those men and women working for our government believe the information that comes from NOAA, the USGS, NASA, colleges and universities, and the World Bank, along with compiled research of ancient writing of the Egyptians, the Mayans and other ancient or lost civilizations.

Through daily updates, our government continues to prepare for all possible scenarios, such as skyscraper-size asteroids that pass by on what is called a "Near Earth Object" (NEO) and any armada of spatial debris that may be in tow, to an actual strike. The government also prepares for a larger spatial object, like Nibiru, whose size could cause gravitational wars with the Sun and trigger an onslaught of solar storms; or the annual increase of volcanic activity around the "Ring of Fire" located in the Pacific that includes several life-on-earth killer super-volcanoes. The government even looks out for things such as the increase of the earth's average temperature and how it affects the weather and the additional appearances of super storms. If you or I were affected by one of these concerns, it could be a life-changing experience. If all of them arrived in a domino effect, we could honestly think Armageddon is upon us because life as we know it may end.

Now, you have a basic understanding of what concerns our government. Our government's survival plans do not include you and me. The survival of your family is your responsibility. Are you ready?

Solar Storms

Nasty is the only reality that describes a solar storm. In terms of the human race and the electrically powered infrastructure that shapes our daily lives, there is no positive message here. That is why you need to become familiar with the following contents of the witches' brew of a solar storm.

- *Gamma Radiation* causes serious damage when absorbed by living cells.
- *X-Ray Radiation* is an ionizing radiation that can cause DNA damage, mutation and death.
- *Ultraviolet (UV) Radiation* is the most dangerous variant of UV light. Prolonged exposure can result in acute and chronic health problems on the skin, in the eyes, and in the immune system.
- *Electromagnetic Pulse (EMP)*, while devastating to electronic devices, passes harmlessly through living cells.
- *Coronal Mass Ejection (CME)* is a giant cloud of heated, electrified gas called "plasma" that erupts from the corona of the Sun. For the most part, CMEs are primarily a threat to satellites, spacecraft, and astronauts, and can disrupt communications on Earth. A CME impact upon the outer part of the Earth's magnetic field could create a worldwide magnetic disturbance, thereby causing violent weather and radiation storms and power outages.

How serious is this? In March of 2006, NASA issued a Solar Storm Warning: not for 2006, but for 2012. NASA explained in the warning that sun spot activity will increase dramatically in 2010–11 and they forecast massive solar storm activity for 2012. Our government is ready—are you?

Acts of Terrorism

Another issue our government has added to their arsenal of survival plans is a set of steps to protect government officials from the threat of future terrorist acts. This threat is very real today and it would behoove us to prepare. At the same time, I am not suggesting we become paranoid, but rather add this possibility to our individual survival plans. In survival, the big key is being prepared. If you have your equipment ready and your mind prepared, your chances of survival are greatly increased. Also, you are usually much more comfortable when you prepare.

When acts of terror occur, they usually happen when we least expect them. The surprise comes from the fact that we have lived pretty safe lives in the past, and also because terrorists plan it that way for maximum effect. The less suspicious people are of an act of violence, the greater the social, mental, and moral damage. This is especially true of the psychological effects of fear. Remember the terrible feelings we experienced when we first heard of the attack on the World Trade Center? Most of us felt deep shock, confusion, anger, and deeply profound fear. Those feelings are exactly the types of psychological responses a terrorist hopes to achieve with an attack.

When we develop our individual survival plans, we need to add the possibility of terrorism to our list, because most professionals who deal with terrorists will tell us that it is only a matter of time before we are subject to more attacks. An attack could affect our water supply, our fresh foods, and even the air we breathe. As the attack on New York demonstrated, terrorists have a very vivid imagination. A terrorist attack could consist of any conceivable weapon at any location. So what can we do to prepare our homes and loved ones if something should happen?

Start getting ready now—not tomorrow. Remember, a terrorist attack will most likely happen when you least suspect it. Take a look around your home: Do you have special clothing, canned foods, and first aid items? What about a battery- or self-powered radio? Or other things that could be placed in storage for emergency use? Don't become paranoid and act like a consumer survivalist. Instead, stop, take a deep breath and think things through.

Volcanic Eruptions

The first thing you need to do is understand what a volcano is. Simply put, a volcano is a vent through which molten rock escapes to the surface of the earth. A volcanic eruption happens when pressure from gases within the molten rock becomes too great. There may be lava flows, poisonous gases, flying rock, and ash. The surrounding landscape may be flattened by the concussion of the initial volcanic explosion.

Because of their intense heat, lava flows are great fire hazards. Lava flows destroy everything in their path, but most move slowly enough that people can move out of the way.

Fresh volcanic ash, made of pulverized rock, can be abrasive, acidic, gritty, gassy, and odorous. While not immediately dangerous, the acidic gas and ash can cause lung damage to infants, older adults, and individuals with severe respiratory illnesses.

Volcanic eruptions can be accompanied by other natural hazards, including earthquakes, mud flows, flash floods, rock falls, landslides, acid rain, fire, and tsunamis. Even a volcano that is thought to be inactive can suddenly erupt. Pay attention to any reports of volcanic activity, and be prepared to move your loved ones to a safe haven.

Asteroid Strikes

Asteroids, like comets, are really just chunks of flying debris left over from the formation of the solar system about 4.5 billion years ago. The ones we are concerned with are the NEOs, and the term "near" is a pretty relative one, since it refers to space debris within a third of the distance to the sun that pose a threat to all nations. For instance, a reasonably large asteroid of 600 feet (200 meters) in diameter crashing into the Atlantic Ocean could create a tsunami that would sink both Britain and the entire East Coast of the United States within minutes.

When we look back at the tracking history of asteroids, we find little of it because until the 1970s, there was actually little interest in asteroids, and NEOs. They were considered little more than low-class astronomical objects. Things began to change in the late 70s when a small but increasing number of astronomers, interested in asteroids, began to be concerned by the abundance of these objects passing close to the Earth. They instituted processes to catalog the asteroids accidentally seen on telescopic plates that had not previously been recorded.

With the intervention of computer models, astronomers learned that the combined gravitational pull of the inner planets caused a sizeable number of asteroids from the Main Asteroid Belt between Mars and Jupiter to cascade down into lower orbits, with many approaching earth. Further, a significant fraction of comets passing thru the inner solar system would be diverted into orbits near earth, due to gravitational encounters with the inner planets. As a result of these discoveries, the estimated number of NEOs increased by about 1000 times.

What does that mean to us? If an asteroid at least one kilometer in size hit the earth, it would cause a dust cloud that would block the sunlight for at least a year, and would lead to a deep worldwide winter and exhaust food supplies (the latter is what caused the dinosaur extinction). Many scientists estimate the initial impact of a single 1 km object could kill up to a quarter of our planet's population.

Smaller hits, about 300 to 600 feet (100 to 200 meters), are far more common. Unfortunately for research, their effect doesn't show up much in global geologic histories. It is estimated, however, that such hits have created many local tsunamis and brief climate changes in recorded history, without any understanding of their cause at the time.

Luckily, Earth's atmosphere gives protection against the vast majority of small asteroids. Asteroids hit the atmosphere at typical speeds in excess of 6 miles per second (10 km per second). Those whose entire orbits reside within the inner solar system hit with an average of about 12 miles per second (20 km per second), with exact relative speed depending upon their angle of approach, and with speeds over 35 miles per second (50 km per second) is common for small cometary objects making a pass from the outer solar system. At this speed, they usually break up due to severe shock pressures, and burn up due to friction with the atmosphere. Think about it: 6 miles per second (10 kilometers per second) is bone-rattling fast—about 22,000 miles (36,000 kilometers) per hour.

For asteroids coming in at 12 miles per second (20 km per second), it's generally thought that to penetrate the atmosphere and cause major damage by tsunami, an iron asteroid must be around 120 to 180 feet (40 to 60 meters) in diameter; a stony asteroid must be 600 feet (200 meters) in diameter. However, a stony asteroid 180 feet (60 meters) in diameter can cause significant damage by explosion due to atmospheric influence. The exact damage inflicted by an asteroid or comet depends upon a number of factors: size, speed, composition of object, and whether it hits land or an ocean.

For a land impact, it can be said that an object of roughly 225 feet (75 meters) in diameter can probably destroy a city; a 480 foot (160 meters) object can destroy a large urban area; a 1050 foot (350 meters) object can destroy a small state; and a 2,100 foot (700 meters) object can destroy a small country.

Smaller objects can cause far more widespread damage with an ocean impact. The effects of an ocean impact are felt much farther away than the effects of an air burst, due to the more effective generation of water waves, and the fact that human populations and big businesses are largely concentrated in coastal cities.

A Warning from the Past

Of the many ancient documents being studied, the following passages referring to the return of Nibiru that was written over 3000 years ago by the Egyptians left the greatest impression with me:

> When blood drops upon the Earth, the Destroyer [Nibiru] will

appear, and the mountains will open up and belch forth fire and ashes. Trees will be destroyed and all living things engulfed. Waters will be swallowed up by the land, and the seas will boil.

The Heavens will burn bright red; there will be a copper hue over the face of the land, followed by a day of darkness. A new moon will appear and break up and fall.

The people will scatter in madness. They will hear the trumpet and battle cry of the Destroyer and will seek refuge within the Earth. Terror will eat away their hearts, and their courage will flow from them like water from a broken pitcher. They will be eaten up in the flames of wrath and consumed by the breath of the Destroyer.

—The Kolbrin: Manuscripts 3:4–6

Time Is the Critical Element

When dealing with all man-made and natural disasters, the more advanced notice we have, the greater our chances for survival. And the experts agree that time is the critical element which can make all the difference in the world of survival.

Face Your Fears

The majority of the human race is so caught up in their daily lives and daily stresses, they honestly think, "Survival planning is something I won't need." Every day, people find themselves dealing with the havoc wreaked by Mother Nature. How do they handle it? Instead of stopping and thinking, most people panic. When you panic, you create within you a sudden state of uncontrollable fear or anxiety that results in irrational behavior and poorly considered decisions. And to panic in a natural disaster can cause death to fall upon you and those who depend on you.

Dealing with Fear

Fear is one of the first reactions to the conscious realization that you are actually a victim of a natural disaster or stranded away from home, due to the same. It is fear that causes many people to panic soon after they realize that they are in a potential survival situation. It is fear that makes people run and discard prepared plans and needed survival equipment.

The following is research that shows us what most people fear in a survival situation:

- **Ridicule or embarrassment**—Those interviewed shortly after being rescued said this was the first fear they experienced. This is especially prominent in experienced outdoorsmen who have a plan and want to maintain a "Daniel Boone" image. They think they can put their ego aside and get into a survival mode
- **Punishment**—It is this fear that causes many lost children and senior citizens to hide soon after they realize they are lost.

Coupled with this concern is the fear of being late. Most of us live daily lives as slaves to a clock, and automatically assume we will face some sort of punishment if we aren't where we need to be when we need to be there. This fear of punishment is present in every survival situation.

- **Being alone**—Many people, including experienced outdoorsmen, have never been truly alone. To them this is a strange and suddenly frightening experience. And for those who have already experienced this, they note that being alone in a room or other such circumstances didn't even come close to the shocking realization of having to survive alone.
- **Animals**—Many people have hidden fears of wild animals and sounds in the woods. Many formerly lost survivalists, especially lost children, mention the fear of wild animals. Most people forget that under the stress of survival, wild animals prefer to avoid people. With a few rare exceptions, wild animals don't usually attack people.
- **Discomfort**—We are so accustomed to comfort, the idea we may get cold, hungry or thirsty, or have to sleep on the hard ground can cause panic. In order to survive, you must accept some discomfort and remember that this is necessary for you to live the rest of your life. This should motivate you to try and build a comfortable survival camp. Learning to cope with discomfort may save your life.
- **The unknown**—All of us live in a fairly predictable day-to-day world. We generally know what we expect to happen both daily and hourly. When we find ourselves suddenly in a survival situation, this comfort of knowing is quickly converted into the fear of the unknown—What should I do now? Will I survive? Will I die? All these unknowns rush through the mind and cloud common sense. This fear is a normal reaction, but the sooner you overcome it and put your survival plan into action, the better. Mentally accept your situation by telling yourself, "Yes, there are many unknowns, but I can't worry about them now because I have a camp to make. I'm also going to have a great story to tell when all of this is over."
- **Darkness**—One of the most common fears, even though many will not admit it, is the fear of the darkness in the open outdoors.

I have seen many brave men admit (privately) that they fear a dark night in the woods or open outdoors. It always amazes me that these same people are not afraid of a dark street in a large city where danger is always nearby, but they are almost paralyzed with fear in the woods at night. There is little to hurt anyone in the darkness of night, whether in the woods or open outdoors, if you stay in one location. To panic and start walking or, worse, running in the dark, can lead to serious injuries. Other than your own imagination, there is little at night that will harm you. So just stay in your survival camp and get a good night's sleep.

Controlling Fear

We all have some, or all, of the above-mentioned fears when we find ourselves in a survival emergency. However, those who get control of their fears quickly and move on and deal with what is at hand are the people that come out of the situation in good shape. Here is how you can cope and live with fear during your survival experience:

1. Don't run away from fear. Admit and accept fear as a normal reaction.
2. Even when you are afraid, act to accomplish the necessities of selecting a campsite, constructing a shelter, getting a small fire going, and preparing to sleep comfortably. Be enthusiastic for your own sake and for the sake of your loved ones.
3. Accept the mind-set of "this has happened to me and I am going to survive." Hope for the best and prepare for the worst.
4. Stay busy. Idleness leads to negative thinking and hopelessness.
5. Practice your religion.
6. Keep a positive attitude.
7. Share all of the previously discussed coping skills with your family—especially with your children and older adults.
8. Continue to remind everyone that "We are alive!" And work to stay that way.

Emotional Acceptance

Acceptance is not finding someone to blame in a survival situation, it starts with your initial emotional reaction to the disaster. It is an individual process through the following stages:

- **Denial**—The refusal to admit or even acknowledge the present situation. It is also known as negation, which is a primitive emotional defense to denounce the existence of an unpleasant reality. During this phase, you should keep an eye on each other because some could slide into a stage of shock.

- **Anger**—The strong need to find the cause of or to assign blame for the present reality. In a disaster that affects the whole populous of the United States, the initial reaction is one of deep and justified anger directed against someone or something unworthy (like the government). Help those you love who are caught in this emotional stag to try and see beyond the present situation by focusing on the day-to-day survival process.
- **Bargaining**—The attempt to rationalize why the present reality happened and to intellectualize any possible way it could have been prevented; or at least reduce the catastrophic affects. Some people will want to return home, or try to come to some type of agreement if they are allowed to return home to what's left of their original life. They will even promise that they will be okay, and that life will return to normal if given a chance. Also, in this stage some people will slide back into denial.
- **Acceptance**—The act of assenting or believing the present situation has actually happened. When a person shows even the slightest acknowledgment that the disaster has truly happened, is a very positive sign. But the person is not completely out of the woods yet. Some people use crying as a coping mechanism in this phase. Crying is okay for women *and* men. And some people in this emotional stag may retreat back into denial.
- **Resolution**—The process of resolving or separating personal perceptions from the present situation.

Some people will pass through the process, some people—like the ones who always seem to land on their feet—could actually skip the whole process because of the demand the present situation has placed upon them. And others will take all the time they need.

Don't waist valuable time pampering the people in your group. Use the buddy system to ensure everyone is moving along, because you have a life or death situation to deal with. Be considerate and gently exert what is called "tough love." Your group has a destination to reach and they are depending on you to get them there safely. Be objective. Do your best to see the disaster exactly for what it is, and keep moving.

A Will to Live

Once you get over the initial shock of being in a survival situation, put a high value on your life and capitalize on your will to live. You will be amazed at what it will get you through. Then continue to think positive as you help your loved ones deal with their fears.

There are many ways to help yourself and your loved ones overcome fear. Ask people to sing a favorite song and encourage all to join in. Others may know several good jokes. And sometimes, the use of old sayings could help. One that comes to my mind is the old axiom "hit the ground running." Not everyone will understand its meaning, giving yet another reason to share. Explain that this saying was first coined in the twentieth century and was used to explain how some people always manage to find themselves in new situations and then instinctively get off to a successful start. For example, hobos jumping from freight trains to explore new towns, or airborne troops being dropped by parachute into hostile territory. Whatever method you use to create a will to live, the first step in "hitting the ground running" is a survival concept called "situational awareness."

Situational Awareness

In essence, Situational Awareness (SA) is a 3-step process by which you quickly assess whatever situation you find yourself in so that you can respond accordingly.

1. What is happening and why?
2. What will happen next?
3. What are my options?

Keep your mind on track and see the situation for what it is. Be flexible and continue at a group pace for your safe haven—and trust your intuition.

Trust Your Intuition

When we do not have the luxury of time for rational thinking, a more intuitive approach can easily mean the difference between life and death.

Each one of us has this inner voice, and we use many different names to define it, such as subconscious, guardian angel, spirit guide, sixth sense, and so forth. For the purpose of this discussion, let's call it good, old-fashion intuition—or gut feeling. The key to make it work effectively is to be willing to trust your instinct enough to forego the sense of control (your ego) that comes with rational thinking.

When the circumstances you are in move faster than you can process them, or when they are difficult to discern, connect with your emotions. But know the difference between emotions that are driven by wounded ego, greed, or pride and set them aside. Focus solely on those emotions that stem from pure instinct.

For example, if you have to make a fast decision and one of the options that looks right does not feel right, go with what feels right. More often than not, what feels right will be the correct choice.

Be Open-minded

In the years to come, we shall come to know fear that is yet unknown to most of us in the twenty-first century. If a catastrophe happens that destroys our life as we know it, we will have more than personal fear to deal with.

Creature comforts of today will no longer exist. Nor will there be hospitals stocked with antibiotics, painkillers, and other marvels of science we've become so accustom to. Rather, we'll be living in a world where people will die of simple infections—if they do not starve to death first.

While vengeance and shoot-outs are stupid ways to get killed, there will be situations where conflict will be unavoidable. If that happens, get mad-dog mean: hit hard, hit fast, and then melt away. Otherwise, always take extreme steps to avoid conflict wherever and whenever possible.

Guidelines to Follow

1. Face your fears and accept them for what they truly are.
2. Trust your intuition—if you cannot trust your intuition, you'll be lost.
3. If you lose your ability to feel compassion for the needy and vulnerable, you are lost.
4. If you lose your ability to love and to be loved, you will remain lost.

No matter how much pain and suffering you endure, never allow yourself to lose your inner moral compass. And through all of this, always protect yourself and your ability to survive.

Time to Prepare

Based on the numerous computer models from the various science and government agencies, anything is possible: solar storms, asteroid strikes, super storms, earthquakes, tsunamis, volcanic eruptions, economic downfall, and even terrorism. As current events become more radical, one of the major signs of change will be the large retail stores struggling to cope with economic fluctuations and the problems that vacillation inflict upon the retail market. And the conveniences that retail stores provide us each day will change drastically over time. When that happens, let us hope we have already started to prepare for the possibilities of our future. If not, and you survive the initial disaster, it is highly possible you and your loved ones will slowly die as victims of the present situation with all the others who thought a survival plan was something they would not need.

What to Expect

As the price of crude oil continues to rise, driving up the price of gasoline and diesel fuel at the pumps, all aspects of our economy will be affected. Unfortunately, most people will only grumble as the cost of filling gas tanks continue to rise, never seeing the connections of gas prices and its effect on the availability of retail store items. Retail store resources will slowly decrease as vast amounts of wood and petrochemical resources used by department and grocery stores to create colorful packaging becomes too expensive to sustain. The result is that we'll see fewer goods on shelves, and many will be packaged very simply or have no packaging at all.

As natural disasters begin to take their toll, the repercussions will affect every link in the supply chain between manufactures and the stores in our communities as natural disasters begin to take their toll. Unlike the fluid and speedy transport system of today, moving goods to stores will become increasingly difficult.

As the petroleum-dependent transportation networks that all retailers depend upon fail, the larger retailers will be forced to move from smaller towns and communities to larger cities. In the process, their employees will join the ranks of the unemployed.

Only when things are in their darkest hour will the powerful grip of the oil interests be broken, and then we could see the emergence of several breakthrough technologies that have long been suppressed—no doubt revealed by the same energy and mining companies that have kept them locked up in their vaults for decades.

As soon as these new alternative power technologies becomes available, people will buy them and find ways to make knock-offs for much less and then sell them locally to their friends and neighbors. Most likely, they'll be selling them from inexpensive stalls in an old retail store that was abandoned and then claimed by the city for back taxes. Likewise, people will also be running their own home businesses to help them get through the economic contractions.

Economic Downfall

We have become so accustomed to our every day conveniences that we would never expect electrical companies to stop making electricity. And we will speak of the "good old days" as we deal with the price of goods that double, quadruple, and then quadruple again. At first, merchants will see this as a great day—their cash registers are full and their products are moving out the door faster than they can replenish the shelves. Eventually reality will sink in as the financial structure crumbles. Not because of any one specific thing, rather by many small things such as the paralysis of the United States mail. Fear, and the fear of panic buying and selling will cause the World Stock exchanges to close. The Federal Reserve Bank will suggest the closure of clearinghouses and corresponding banks as a precaution. Traveler's checks, personal checks, and even government savings bonds will become worthless paper. And your savings account will be sealed for your own financial safety, leaving you with only the cash money in your pocket.

Like most small towns throughout the United States, the merchants rely upon food and drug supplies delivered daily, or even thrice weekly from warehouses in the larger cities. Each day tank trucks replenished the many gas stations. For all other merchandise, the communities are dependent upon shipments by mail, express, and highway freight, from jobbers and manufacturers elsewhere.

In a disaster, all these services will halt entirely and it will seem to happen all at once. From that moment, the communities and the people will have to subsist on whatever was already within its boundaries—plus what they might scrounge from the countryside. There will be runs on tires, coffee, sugar, cigarettes, butter, the choice cuts of beef, and nylon stockings (very useful for many things). Slowly, merchants will see the end before them and try to slow things down by instituting their own rationing systems. And by the end of the day, scarcity will condemn the once all-mighty dollar to degradation and contempt. Within a few more days, the dollar could be banished entirely as a medium of exchange and many will say this ban will be only temporary—at least for the duration. In its place will raise a different exchange.

Bartering System

Venders will appear overnight, setting up 10x10 foot booths in deserted retail stores, along main street, in vacant lots, and in your and my garage. We will trade services in exchange for goods that we can either use or barter. The exchange rate will be personal—haggled out in a sport of words by desperate tongues and people with empty stomachs. It might not be the best process at first but over time, a "fair trade" system will surface. Venders will prove to the world that having more does not give you the right to callously exploit those who have less. This will be the beginning of neighbor caring for neighbor and people helping people, and each person's abiding respect for the dignity of life will enable all of us to create the kind of survival communities needed to face the tribulations ahead.

With that said, now it's time to plan ahead.

Home Business

The nightly news is full of stories concerning change. The outcome of these changes will inevitably have an adverse affect on our economy. Wondering what our government, big businesses, or the financial institutions are going to do about this is pointless.

Your time will be better spent building a small home-based business or trade that can be operated under a barter system and that can change and flex with the turbulent time ahead. A Master's degree is not required—anyone can do it! To help illustrate the point, the following examples show the simplicity of three different possible startup home businesses.

Gardening—Do you enjoy growing plants? Congratulations! You've got the making of a home business. Start today. Check out garage sales for bargains on gardening tools while they're still cheap and plentiful. Build a seed bank with species that will grow in a diverse range of temperatures and conditions. Check out the new and used book stores for books on gardening, home-made fertilizers, bug and pest control, and other remedies that may be helpful.

The basics, such as cabbage, carrots, potatoes, peas, corn, and herbs for flavoring will always be in demand. So will flowers (most of which are edible) that can be used to brighten up windowsills and then steeped to make nourishing mugs of tea or herbal poultices. Even in time of turmoil, we'll still want to gossip, and sharing a cup of tea with a friend or a neighbor is good for the soul.

Sewing—During a survival situation, we're not going to have the time to worry about being fashionable; rather we will be concerned with just keeping the fashion we've got on our backs. This is why a good tailor or seamstress will be worth their weight in gold.

If you've got the latest computerized sewing machine with all the great stitching patterns, lucky you. Enjoy it while the electricity is still available, because in the future, it will not. When the lights go out, your fancy sewing machine will be dead as a doorknob. At that point, you're sewing everything by hand and that is a hard way to make a survivable living—but there's a better way.

Today, while they're still available and relatively cheap, buy an old, turn-of-the-century foot pedal sewing machine. Acquire two, or perhaps three of them, and have them professionally serviced. Also, see if you can locate spare parts, then pack them safely away.

While sewing supplies are still cheap, stock up on needles, thread, zippers, measuring tapes, and so forth. Search the closeout sales on cloth, and collect a large selection of clothing from rummage sales; today's out-of-fashion, is tomorrow's go-to-town outfit. Collect non-colorful fashions so they will not attract the wrong attention. People will want durable clothes with the comfort of natural fibers and the reliability of strong fasteners. Above all, make sure the clothing has lots of pockets, as we'll be scavenging a lot more in the years to come.

Candles—Are you a person who enjoys making decorative candles in your spare time? You may already have the making of an excellent home business.

Beeswax or paraffin, wicks, and candle molds are still inexpensive and readily available, so start stocking up. Likewise, stock up on boxes of safety matches while they're still cheap. While you're at it, start learning how to make your own candles from scratch, using anything that could work as a replacement (rendered fats, processed oils, and so forth). Instead of decorating candles on the weekends, make them from scratch in every possible way; test them to see how they perform. From one of my experiences, crayons, both old type and new, do not work very well. It is best to learn what works and what doesn't work while mistakes are still cheap.

Start Today

I hope the three examples above will excite your imagination. Don't fall for the concept that the examples appear to be for women—the same holds true for men. Stop, look around, and allow your imagination to envision the unlimited possibilities. Case in point: if you're a good mechanic, you can start finding old bicycles frames and matching them up with serviceable car alternators and make foot powered electrical generators.

While you are out hunting for items, frequent the thrift shops for a manual typewriter in good condition. Have it serviced and then buy fabric ribbons and ink. Seal them up for safekeeping along with blank labels for your merchandise. Likewise, if you load your own ammunition, stock up on surplus ammo, primers, powders, and other necessities. People will need reliable firearms and ammunition to protect their families. Then, pack up everything you've gathered to start your home business, and store it somewhere safe and dry.

Assuming the worst happens, is planning and stockpiling supplies a pointless exercise? Absolutely not! At this point in time, you're not living in that dark future scenario and you have the luxury of time—use it wisely.

Developing a Survival Plan

Survivors begin surviving by first sitting down quietly and contemplating that which could happen. For consumers, this seems like a silly waste of time—especially when you know there is a freshly stocked bunker under your gazebo and a shiny new 4x4 in the driveway.

A Survival Planning Program

The survivalist already knows what every military planner expects. Once the shooting happens, all good plans go out the door because events on the ground dictate the rules. This is why military planners spend so much time visualizing the battlefield in their mind through war games. By doing this, they create a framework of ideas and concepts that will enable them to rapidly and decisively respond to what will become a fluid and fast-moving situation. After they feel they've identified as many variables as possible, they know what they need, and they go shopping.

There is another benefit to thinking in this manner. As you create various ideas and concepts of survival, you also create new neural networks in your brain; in a literal sense, you wire your brain to perform in these circumstances. In order to make this process work, you must visualize yourself dealing with all of the variables in this survival scenario.

If you are serious about surviving the catastrophes most likely to fall upon you, as well as those you'd never expect in your wildest dreams, now is the time to use your imagination like a war gamer.

Identify as many threats and threat combinations as you can that could befall your geographical area and that make sense to you. Take into account the havoc an Electromagnetic Pulse (EMP) will have on the unshielded electronic computer systems in the warehouses, stores, planes, trains and automobiles, and the cascading affect that will have on transporting supplies across our country. Then, find a quiet place where you can be alone with your thoughts and use your imagination to explore each scenario one by one. In that process, do not forget the possibility of a lazy neighbor whose plan is to rob you when the time comes.

Close your eyes and use your imagination; begin by seeing yourself doing whatever you do in the course of a normal day. Then imagine the event. Perhaps it begins with sirens and the sight of coworkers fleeing the building. Or perhaps you're having a BBQ in the backyard with your family when you begin to feel the earth shake deep beneath your feet.

As the visualization unfolds, see yourself responding to what is happening. Be honest in evaluating your response. If you see yourself not knowing what to do, make a mental note of that and find the information you need on the Internet or through local agencies to fill that gap.

Once you have the information you need in hand, it's useless to you until you have it in mind. So find a quiet place, and use your imagination to run through the scenario again. Once you honestly feel that you see yourself handling this particular scenario, play it through to the next day, the next week, the next month, and so on. In your scenario, remember that you and your loved ones will be a small group among the millions of people trying to survive. You will be dealing with mother nature, the efforts and failures of local, state and federal government agencies, and of bad people doing bad things (discussed in detail in chapter 11).

Also keep in mind that there are no absolutes in this life. The things discussed in this book are only relative references to the numerous tribulations big business and governments have taken stock of that could affect all of us over a period of years. You too must think of it in that context.

Personalizing the Survival Planning Program

Another aspect of all this is that each of us creates our individual survival plans in our own way. There is no "one-size-fits-all" approach to this. After you work through your first scenario, tweak the process in a way that makes the plan feel right to you. Also, find a pace that does not interrupt your life, but one you can follow on a consistent basis.

Although this form of contemplation would appear to be depressing, what you will begin to feel is a strong sense of empowerment that will help offset the weight of a catastrophe that might otherwise catch you unprepared and on the run because you relented to the old adage of "I'll wait and see."

I'll Wait and See

When the old colloquialism nags at you to put dreary thoughts aside and to dwell on more pleasant thoughts, stop and think before you say to yourself "I'll wait and see," or "God will take care of me." While you are thinking, visualize a large bridge in your mind; not the well-maintained bridge of today, but a tattered structure packed with fleeing refugees from railing to railing, an ocean of people virtually impassable that stretches far beyond the military checkpoint you'll have to pass through as well. That is, if they let you.

Again, before you dismiss this, remember back over the last few years and the ever increasing destructive weather patterns and the TV coverage of highways packed with cars trying to retreat at the last minute from the approaching threat. For me, this type of thinking brings back the memory of a story concerning a man who was caught in one of the floods of recent years that plagued the Mississippi valley:

> The man explained to the deputy sheriff that he planned to remain with his home during the approaching flood. As the water rose, he crawled up on the roof. Another deputy came by in a boat and offered him a ride to safety, the man declined, as he explained that God would save him. The waters continued to rise and the man stood on the crown of his roof as the waters lapped at his feet. Another group of people came by in a boat offering him a ride, and again the man explained he was okay because God would save him. The water continued to rise forcing the man to climb to the vary top of his TV antenna tower. The water was up to his shoulders when a helicopter flew by and tried to rescue him. And again the man explained that God would save him. The next thing the man knew, he was standing at the pearly gates of heaven, face to face with God. Immediately he demanded to know why God had not saved him. When he finally stopped ranting and raving, God calmly explained, "I sent four people. What else did you expect me to do?"

Keep this in mind the next time you find yourself discussing survival plans with your friend and he says, "I'll wait and see," or "I'll let God take care of it." If you still feel the urge to explain the finer points of the need to plan ahead to them, ignore it. Your friend is still in denial, and if you press the point, they'll likely close down even more and say something like, "I haven't the time for this!"

The best thing to do is share what you know, take a deep breath and remind yourself: survival is a personal responsibility. Then continue your process of preparing.

The 8–18 Solar Storm Plan

The reason I referred to a solar storm as nasty is because it is a witch's brew of several ingredients that will happen very fast. Eight minutes after the solar storm erupts from the Sun, gamma radiation from the solar flare begins penetrating your body. High levels of X-Ray and UV radiation will shortly follow that. And maybe even an EMP explosion in the upper atmosphere. This deadly shower can last up to three hours. Eighteen hours later, the Coronal Mass Ejection starts to slam into Earth's magnetic fields and may trigger violent weather and radiation storms.

Before most ordinary citizens comprehend what is happening, our leaders will already be safely underground because of the early warning system designed into our government's survival plan. Their shelters will be well hardened against solar storm dangers, with equally survivable electronics and communication and environmental systems.

As for you and me, the first step in our 8–18 Solar Storm Plan is to pay attention. We hope the Emergency Broadcast System will warn us beforehand on both radio and TV. Another way is for us to be observant when we see the following: people rushing out of homes or business to look at the sky, the Sun becoming brighter, and/or our cell phones losing all signal. When these things happen, it is time for you to find an underground safe-zone. Utilize whatever you have on hand as you run toward a protective shelter: hat, umbrella, sunglasses, folded newspaper, blanket, coat, and other items you find in the safety kit in the trunk of your car.

- Protection at home:
  - » safe rooms
  - » storm shelters
  - » root cellars
  - » basements
- Protection in cities:
  - » underground parking garages
  - » auto and pedestrian tunnels
  - » underground subway systems

  - tall buildings with deep basements
  - banks with open vaults
  - catacombs
  - sewage systems
  - storm drains
- Protection in the country:
  - any cave
  - any mine
  - any tunnel
  - road culverts
  - roadway tunnels
  - cliff overhangs
  - natural stone arches

Unlike tornadoes or severe storms that slam into you from the side, a solar storm comes directly from the sun, down at you. Remember that and start looking around today for safe havens, and hone this skill with practice.

Volcanic Eruption Plan

After living 21 kilometers west of Mount Pinatubo in the Philippines and experiencing the chaos of its eruption in 1991, I hope I will never go through another, but by living near Yellowstone, I know that possibility lies ahead. At the same time, even though I know what could happen, it still behooves me to prepare. The best place to start is to ask questions:

- **What can I do before a volcanic eruption?** Add a pair of goggles and a disposable breathing mask to your survival kit or backpack for each member of your family. If you have the time, stay away from the immediate area of an active volcano site and find out how wide the initial blast radius will be.
- **What do I do during a volcanic eruption?** If you have the time to evacuate, immediately leave the volcano area to avoid flying debris, hot gases, lateral blast, and lava flows. To miss the imitate danger of mud flows, avoid river valleys and low-lying areas.
- **What kind of protection do I need for falling ash?** It is very important to protect yourself from volcanic ash. Accomplish that by wearing long-sleeved shirts and long pants. Use goggles and wear eyeglasses instead of contact lenses. Use a dust mask, several #4 coffee filters, or hold a damp cloth to cover your face,

help with breathing, and protect your lungs. Then, if possible, stay away from areas downwind from the volcano to avoid volcanic ash. The best thing to do is stay indoors until the ash has settled unless there is a danger of the roof collapsing. Close doors, windows, and all ventilation in the house. Remember, volcanic ash is very fine rock pumice that can cause damage to lungs, eyes, machinery, and automobile engines. Therefore, avoid running cars, trucks, or generator engines. If you have to drive, keep your speed under 35 miles per hour.

- **What do I do after a volcanic eruption?** Can you remain in your home? Or do you need to evacuate? Where do you go? Now it is time to put your survival plan into action. Take care of yourself and your loved ones.

A Walkout Plan

We discussed the emotional acceptance and practical things you can do to stockpile inexpensive survival provisions and supplies for your home business.

These are things you can do today, but what happens to all your provisions and business supplies if a disaster makes your town or city uninhabitable? Likewise, how can you possibly transport all of the goods to another area when the roads are gridlocked with abandoned and derelict autos, or with bandits and pirate gangs roaming the countryside looking for people like you?

In the coming years, all of us will have to contend with the same types of catastrophes we experience now, but under very different circumstances. They will happen with greater frequency, be more intense overall, and strike unannounced in completely new areas. The result is that the very nature of how we cope with these catastrophes will change.

Need for a Walkout Plan

One solution is to have a walkout plan and all it entails ready so that when disaster strikes, you can lead your loved ones to a safe haven. This new reality shall be very different from how we plan for disasters today. To understand that difference, we must begin by looking at how the entire populace currently views disaster management.

First, we need to think beyond a 3-day survival solution, because the worst will be worse than any disaster we have faced to date.

Those who have researched this topic for years have labored hard to predict which areas of what country will be safe havens in the years to come, and which will become uninhabitable or simply gone altogether.

In the United States, moving to safe areas such as the mountains is reasonably good advice. Nevertheless, picking up and moving away from home is easier said than done. Consequently, we must face the possibility that we may have to move at some future date. But for now, that idea is just a plan; for life is good right where we are.

As you build your plan, take into count your local terrain, your proximity to waterways, flood plains, land and water fault lines, the possibility of volcanic activity, and the ring of fire. You also need to account for the possibility of multiple ocean and land asteroid strikes where water and dirt will be blasted into the atmosphere, causing many weeks of rain, raining mud, and little to no sunlight. That could also lead to temperature drops and an early snowfall in the mountains in the summer or heavier snowfall in the winter.

Creating a Walkout Plan

The very first thing you must do when creating a walkout plan is to decide where you're going to walk to. This destination must be an area that you feel, with a comfortable level of confidence, will survive the most likely catastrophes. For example, if you live in an area prone to flooding, find a nearby area that is well above the flood plain.

Because there are so many variations on these possibilities, you'll have to do some research on your own. If you live in an area where you know you will need a walkout plan, you must do it before you:

- organize your home business;
- stockpile safe haven supplies;
- create your walkout plan;
- purchase walkout gear and supplies; and
- get in good enough physical shape to walk to your destination.

In terms of getting through the years to come, the 3-day disaster plans currently practiced, and ill-conceived survival shopping sprees will only put you in harms way. This is because you must first decide on where your walkout haven will be. Once this question is settled, the *how* and *when* become obvious.

Choosing Your Walkout Haven

Most people will end up walking out, so choose your destination wisely. While things are stable, use the time to gather and transport your survival provisions and survival business supplies to a safe haven.

Storing these invaluable provisions and supplies in an area that is likely to become uninhabitable is pointless. Therefore, the obvious immediate choice for a walkout haven is the home of a close friend or family member, someone with whom you share a warm and trusting relationship.

Likewise, if you're a retired grandparent, finding such an area and moving there for the benefit of your children and grandchildren will be tough at first. Short-term, you'll leave a network of friends behind, and even better medical care in some cases. Long-term, the wisdom of your years will allow you to see your beloved ones alive and well in a world gone mad with disaster.

If you cannot create trustworthy relationships with others in your intended walkout haven, another option is to rent a locker in a secure facility and store your things there. Share this location on a need-to-know basis with others.

Regardless of your safe haven arrangements, stock it with plenty of hand tools such as picks and shovels. You'll not only need to begin growing your own food, you'll also need to prepare and maintain solar radiation shelters.

Whether they are underground bunkers, abandoned mines, or natural caves, you'll need a place to go underground when the solar storms begin to batter the Earth.

When the worst comes, you may be able to get part of the way to your safe haven in a car, truck, ATV, or motorcycle, but do not plan on it. Rather, expect to walk all the way and on short notice. For this reason, you need to know how far you can walk in a day and how many days you can stay on your feet before reaching your safe haven. The best way to determine this would be the endurance level of the youngest and oldest members of your group.

Elderly Family Members, Pets, and Livestock

The decisions each of us will need to make pertaining to this subject will be heartbreaking to most. We must decide who will have a chance to make it to safety and who will not. During the family discussion, emotional bonds will cause much pain and outcry from loved ones. But in the end, rational thinking needs to prevail for the safety of all.

- **Elderly family members**—When an elderly person reaches dotage, moving them from their present surrounding could cause more harm than leaving them in the care of the assisted living facility. As a retired counselor with living parents, and children located in several states through the continental United States, this one decision will be the hardest emotional struggle that will have to be faced and balanced with or against the needs and safety of the group.

- **Pets and livestock**—Life is celebrated to its fullest with the inclusion of pets in our family circle. What we need to seriously look at in the planning process are the special needs our pets and livestock require and what it will take to accommodate them. Our food, water, and medical care must include the supplies for pets if we plan to take them with us. Most larger dogs, horses, cattle, and even goats can be fitted with packs to help carry their needs. The smaller species of dogs, cats, and other pets will end up as additional weight, requiring us to carry them to the safe haven. This weight will take the place of other supplies needed by humans. And yes, our children will try to bargain to keep their beloved pet, unaware of the additional stress it will cause. Ask yourself and your loved ones very hard questions: Do we starve a family member to feed a dog or cat? Can we add an additional twenty-five pounds to an already heavy pack? Try to help them see that it would probably be best to release the animals and focus on the family needs first.

Life and death decisions will plague all of us throughout the survival process. Being open and honest in the beginning will help set a standard for all to follow. And as you and your loved ones prepare for the possibilities of the future, to one day actually dealing with the actual disaster and then walkout to your safe haven, always chose the most humane path to survival.

Planning the Walkout Route

When disasters loom far off on the horizon, we often have enough time to gather our loved ones together so that we can hunker down or flee together. Other times, disasters strike with little or no warning at all. When that happens, the first thought most people have is to return home.

Home, or wherever your children might be, will be a natural rally point in any disaster. When loved ones are lost, finding them becomes a nightmare, especially when cellular networks fail.

For this reason, family and friends must develop interlacing systems of rally points that incorporate various scenarios. Besides the natural rally points like homes, schools and day care centers, you will also need a nearby walkout rally point.

If you have teenagers, you will also need to take into account the emotional bonds between your teenagers and their boyfriend or girlfriend, and peers. Sometimes mixing disaster-triggered fear with hormones will distract even the best of intentions of an adolescent teenager. Be an understanding parent and include your teenager in the planning process and make note of his or her feelings and concerns pertaining to friends and peers.

When planning your primary walkout route, remember to always have a plan B—an alternate route you can use in case your first choice is impassable. Remember, your rally points depend on your circumstances and your primary and alternative walkout route choices.

Be prepared for as many issues along the way as you can. For example, if others in your walkout group are straggling behind because their feet are killing them, how long do you make everyone else wait until the stragglers catch up? You'll have to make these types of decisions when developing your walkout plan. Be sure to create a simple signal system of stick figures or stones to mark the trail, that only your group will recognize and use.

Once you've decided your routes and rally points, designate rest points that offer potable water and shelter. This is especially important if your walkout will take two or more days. If possible, take the time to travel your chosen routes and personally inspect all your rally points and rest stops.

Be thorough. The more you know about your routes, such as nearby towns, medical facilities, police stations, bridges, dams, highway tunnels and military bases, the better. Take into account the possibility of a total collapse of order at all of these places and the need for alternate routes. Also, take family and friends on these trips and have them help; involve them in the process of looking for ponds, water tanks, or wells along your walkout route.

Once everything is organized into a complete walkout plan, make sure everyone has a copy with maps, contact information, and so forth sealed in a vinyl cover or within several sealable plastic storage and freezer bags. Now you are ready, right? Not yet.

Vaccinations

When were the last time you checked to see if every family member's vaccinations were up to date? Do not take a chance. Review each person's shot record with your family physician, or if money is an issue, a free community nurse service. Ensure every person's vaccinations are up-to-date, specifically: typhoid, hepatitis A, hepatitis B, tetanus, and MMR (measles, mumps, rubella).

That being accomplished, let's go shopping.

Going Shopping

Now it's time to go shopping for walking gear and supplies. The first thing you'll want to get is a backpack for each family member.

Backpacks for Adults

In a catastrophic setting, the versatile daypacks and backpacks used today by our children at school and college have one particular virtue. Unlike a large bulky hiker backpack with an aluminum frame to make it manageable over long distances, a backpack is ideal for anyone fleeing a catastrophe. Loaded with thirty pounds of provisions and gear, it can be dropped on a moment's notice, used as a shield for self-defense, or easily dragged through tight crawl spaces.

Your backpack is the most important piece of survival gear you'll ever own. This is why putting it together the right way requires careful attention to detail. Always remember that the amount of gear you can lug on your back varies with your age and state of physical fitness and health.

Wherever possible, use multi-functional items. When choosing between two items, lighter is better—as long as it is reliable. In a very real sense, less weight equals more comfort when creating your own custom backpack (and have walked a couple days into your walkout).

The following suggestions for the kind of backpack you need and other food and personal items are solely intended as a starting point. Use the following suggestions as the first step to build your own backpack ounce-by-ounce, while keeping your geographic, seasonal weather variations, types of threats, and personal needs firmly in mind.

Selecting Your Backpack

When it comes to buying a backpack, ignore the back-to-school bargains. Saving a few dollars this way will come back and haunt you with debilitating aches and pains. Visit local sporting good stores and try several different packs on for size. Pay close attention to the parts that come into contact with your body.

The shoulder straps need to be wide, well padded, and easy to slip on and off. Make sure they feel comfortable and fit naturally on your shoulders. Backpacks also come with carry handles at the top center of the bag. Make sure the handle is well stitched, strong, and comfortable in your hand.

The backside of the pack should be padded and comfortable, to keep your back from becoming sweaty and bruised by the contents in the pack. Also, wide web pockets for water jugs are good things to have.

Then ask the clerk if it is okay to stuff a few pounds of goods in the pack and then walk around the store for ten minutes just to make sure it stays comfortable. While you're walking around, check to see if there are other handy lightweight survival items to consider.

If money is still a concern after you have found the type of backpack you want, do not forget about bargain shops and secondhand sporting goods stores.

Backpacks for Kids

Finding backpack for kids can become a great challenge, but do not give up. In the process of picking out a pack for your children, remember the body-length of the pack should not exceed the distance from the shoulder to the hip of your child. For small children, check out the women's purses. Over the years, many manufactures have designed women's purses to look like mini-backpacks. You may luck out and find a pint-size pack for your little one.

Remember, this is a family project, a family process, and a family walkout. Include the children and allow them to choose the clothing that will go into their personal backpack. Limit the weight to relate to the child's age (30 pounds is the average for an adult, do the math), so the kid's pack does not tire the children and create more weight for you to carry.

Non-food Items

Here are a few things to acquire, if you do not already have them:

Compass—As we approach the possible return of Nibiru in 2012 and an increase in solar storm activity, the earth's magnetic field could weaken. Taking an accurate compass heading may become problematic; however, a compass will still be vital. A combination sighting and map compass is best, but a simple compass is just as good.

Survival knife—The best knife would be a high quality, 4-inch fixed carbon blade survival knife, with a wood or rubber grip and a sheath. For those willing to pay a little more, the World War II era 7-inch Marine Ka-Bar knife offers a time-proven design. No matter what you buy, make sure the knife you buy is made with high quality carbon steel.

A folding knife is handy as a backup and for general use, but remember they can break when cutting through something hard.

Hiking staff—Hikers use staffs to help them cross creeks, streams, rivers, and to traverse hillsides. Hiking staffs give extra power and balance while easing wear and tear on knees, hips, and backs. In the future, you'll need them to help navigate broken roads and debris, and to keep hungry animals at bay.

Binoculars—Disasters are always filled with nasty obstacles. The ability to see them at a distance can make all the difference. You can often find good general-purpose or birding binoculars in the 8x30 range on sale or at garage sales. Before you buy any binoculars, try them out. Be sure their view is clear and sharp, they are easy to focus, and they are durable.

Spare reading glasses or magnifier—Many of us wear prescription reading glasses, but sometimes, when we're in a hurry, they can be left behind. Keep a small, inexpensive pair of generic drug store readers in a hard case in your backpack. This way you always can read a map and see a sliver under the skin or an irritating speck in someone's eye. It is also a good idea for those of you who do not need glasses.

Lens cleaning kit—A lens cloth like the one we get with prescription glasses is a must-have in a windy environment filled with dust, pumice, ash, smoke, salts, and other small particles. You may even want a small lens cleaning kit like the ones used by photographers.

32-ounce water bottle—Filling a wide mouth water bottle is faster and easier than most canteens. Make sure your backpack has a side web pocket for a 32-ounce wide-mouth water bottle, and buy a new one when you purchase your pack.

Flat pack water tank—In any disaster, potable water will become a scarce necessity. Keep some kind of foldable water tank in your pack. Make sure it is durable, with heavy seams and a comfortable handle. When dry, most foldable water tanks weigh about 1 ounce for every liter of capacity, so a 6-liter tank will weigh about 6 ounces or less when empty. Other alternative water containers would be the self-sealing plastic bags you carry; the plastic bag in which the tube tent is packed also makes a good water container.

Water purification—There are many myths about water purifying itself in the outdoors. One popular theory is that water, swiftly running over, around, and through rocks purifies itself. Do not believe that. Another myth claims that if clear water sits in the sun for an hour, the germs are killed. Another myth is that water exposed to the sun while cascading down a waterfall will kill all the germs. Again, these are untrue. Therefore, it is your responsibility to treat all water sources found on your walkout. Several common ways are: boiling the water, using Halazone tablets, Potable Aqua tablets, bleach treatment, iodine and betadine treatment, and a microfilter/microbiological water purifier pump. To understand more about each of these methods, read about them in chapter 6 before you go shopping.

All of these are time-tested processes to treat water, but none of them are 100 percent effective. The only surefire way to kill all the nasty things that live in our water today is by boiling the water—when it is safe to use a fire.

Tube tent—It will be nice to have a warm place to go to and get in out of the wind and the elements that also acts as a protective barrier from ground moisture. Plus, a tube tent can double as a raincoat or wrap to keep the body dry and warm in bad weather.

Hooded poncho—A hooded poncho not only provides excellent protection from the rain, snow, and icy winds, but you can also sleep under it like a tarp or sleep on it to protect you from ground moisture. If you are fleeing a volcanic eruption, it will also help you keep pumice from caking to your body and getting in your cloths.

Space blanket—A space blanket is a must-have for emergency protection in all weather. A space blanket also offers protection from UV sunlight during a solar storm. In the event of a nuclear attack, it will keep the nuclear fallout from falling directly on your body, or getting inside your cloths or hair while you evacuate from the fall-out area. Once used for this purpose, you must dispose of the blanket, so keep two or three space blankets in your backpack.

> **Note**—Be prepared for anything you can imagine. On top of all the possibilities that could happen during a catastrophic disaster, do not be surprised if some arrogant human being decided to push the button and start a nuclear war to ensure his or her enemies are completely wiped out.

Iodine tablets—If you find yourself downwind of a nuclear detonation, you can mitigate the effects of radioactive iodine on your thyroid gland by taking potassium iodine anti-radiation pills. These pills essentially fill the thyroid to capacity with normal iodine, so that there is no physical ability for the thyroid to absorb irradiated iodine. Store one tablet for each expected walkout day in each backpack. Include a few extra to allow for unforeseen delays.

Signal mirror—Volcanic ash from volcanic eruptions, ocean water, and dirt flung into the upper atmosphere from asteroids striking the earth will cause global dimming. The skies will become overcast and rainy, eventually clearing to a reddish and black-streaked sky. While this will diminish the light reflected by a signal mirror, this handy device should still be in your backpack.

High-decibel whistle—If you find yourself buried under rubble and your mouth is so dry you can't speak any louder than a whisper, a loud whistle will help someone locate you more quickly.

Renewable energy flashlight—A normal flashlight is good if you are willing to add the weight of extra batteries to your pack. However, the new renewable energy flashlights are more practical for years of use because they never need batteries or light bulbs. You energize them by shaking them, which moves a high-powered magnet back and forth inside a wire coil. Three minutes of shaking can give you about twenty minutes of light.

GI can opener (P-38 or P-51)—Taking side trips during your walkout to forage for canned goods can net you some immediate sources of food and protein. Trying to open those cans with a pocketknife or crude punch is a good way to injure a hand. It is better to find and carry an Army can opener, so you can enjoy your meal and continue on the trail.

GI magnesium fire starter—In terms of a walkout, you only want to start a fire during the day for an emergency. At night, a fire offers safety and warmth. That's when you will appreciate these old Army-issue magnesium block fire starters. They work very well in inclement weather. We'll talk more about this in a later chapter.

Bic-type lighters—Six of these lighters take up about 4x4 inches of space. Individually, one lighter is good for about a thousand lights. Water does not prevent its use. It fits in any pocket and can be used as a temporary emergency light. It is also a good barter object and its flash can scare away animals; but it does not replace the knowledge of how to build a fire.

5-Piece mess kit—Shop around and do not fall for the "aluminum is lighter" gimmick. There are stainless steel mess kits that are light and better quality.

Aluminum foil—This is one of the most versatile items to have in a pack. A 36x36-inch square of foil can become a cooking pot to boil water, cook food, make coffee, or to make a heat reflector for the fire or a signal mirror.

Insect repellent—During times of disaster, there will be a lot of rotting carcasses lying around to spawn insects. To help you transition into living in the outdoors, insect repellent is a must. To help this process, stop using all hand lotions, perfumes, aftershave, and cologne. When the insect repellent eventually runs out, you might need, based on your climate, relief found in the use of the milky juice of dandelion plants. Rub it on and keep on walking.

Parachute cord—Instead of wishing for a small length of rope, add fifty feet of parachute cord to your pack. You will find that it is a valuable item with many purposes. It is especially helpful when anchoring down a shelter. If small, strong string is needed, the parachute cord can be cut open and the many small strings can be used separately to repair clothing, close the end of a tub tent, or even as fishing line.

Wire—For those of you who would like to try trapping small animals for additional food, pack several feet of a small gage wire to make snares. Even if you do not know how, read up on it (discussed in chapter 10) and you will amaze the family when you come back into camp with a couple of rabbits for supper.

Bolt cutter—Cutting a chain, padlock, or fence can save a life. Cutting sheet metal or wire can assist you with camp preparation. It is a little heavy, but worth its weight in gold.

Toilet paper—When you see a half-used roll of toilet paper, replace it with a full roll. Then, compress the old one and put it in a self-sealing plastic bag. When life becomes miserable, it's the little things that help you hang on to your sanity.

Sanitary napkins and tampons—When preparing a female's pack, remember space and weight is critical. If the female is using napkins, think about switching over to tampons. If your period does start while on your walkout, remember that you need to take special precautions with the disposal of your used napkins and tampons. Bury them away from camp to prevent the arrival of unwanted hungry animals drawn by the smell of blood.

> **Note**—Remember earlier we discussed the idea of finding double use for items? Another use for a sanitary napkin is that of a bandage for serious wounds. If the worst would happen and you find yourself or a loved one without store bought sanitary napkins, a natural replacement could be the fur-side of a tanned rabbit pelt or hide. This can be washed out and reused several times.

Folding camp shovel—For adults, a surplus Army field shovel is cheap and sturdy. This item is usually attached to the outside of a backpack. For those with a little more to spend, consider a lightweight, multipurpose folding camp shovel. Not only can they be used to dig holes, it is also a lethal weapon when swung like a club.

> **Note**—The old adage, "Leave the camp area the way you found it," could save a life. You and your family will not be the only ones walking out, and many groups may not be as prepared as you. If you leave evidence of a campsite behind, those less prepared might hunt you down and relieve you of all your possessions. If you do not want that to happen, bury all your discarded items, along with the campfire. Then try your best to return the area to the way it looked before you arrived.

Soap and personal grooming—Ever brought home a few of those little boxes of soap from a hotel? Ensure they are unscented (remember the insects) and seal a few in a plastic bag along with a small nail clipper, toothbrush, and a comb.

> **Note**—It would behoove you to seriously think about leaving all that make-up, facial cream, body lotions, and so forth at home. As life slowly pulls itself up, those things will again become a daily habit. Until then, they can actually cause more harm by preventing your body from adjusting to the outdoors. The perfume can be smelled from a long distance as it drifts upon the wind, drawing not only insects, but also bad people who could cause harm to you and your loved ones.

Sealable plastic bags—If you accidentally dropped your backpack in a river, or if it gets left out in the rain, anything that is not waterproof becomes dead weight. Put *everything* you can into sealable, heavy-duty plastic bags, and save the plastic bags for another day.

#4 coffee filters—Triangle-shaped #4 coffee filters are a must-have in any backpack, because they can filter muddy water. They are also a great way to keep dust and pumice out of your lungs. Expect lots of volcanic eruptions in the years ahead, and when the pumice and ash begin to fall, two #4 filters can keep volcanic pumice from turning into a deadly, glassy cement in your lungs. A sealable plastic bag with twenty or more #4 filters is light, and you'll have enough to share with others. Keep your filters at the top of your pack where they are easy to find or in a zippered pocket on your pack.

Duct tape—Using duct tape is a quick way to patch a tear in a tube tent or poncho, and saves lives time-and-again. You can also use it to tape #4 coffee filters to your face to free your hands. Use it to restrain someone who has become mentally unstable. Use it as a temporary tourniquet to stop a bleeding injury or use it to temporarily immobilize a broken bone or limb as you evacuate a person to safety.

Fishing kit—Many times forgotten, but always remembered later, is the fishing kit. You will need to make your own kit based on your region, needs, and circumstances. Have a variety of fishing hook sizes, lead sinker weights, Styrofoam bobbers, and a 100-foot roll of at least 8# weight of fishing line. All other things are up to you.

Pocket survival guide—Do not forget to place this book in your survival pack; and you need to give all of this a field test. Actually use your survival backpack overnight so you are familiar with everything dealing with your walkout plan and you will be ready when you need to walkout.

Pocket medical herbal guide—You need to find a pocket-size herbal medicine guide. It is very important the pocket guide has actual color pictures of each herbal plant to help you recognize each one. Then take it on a test walk. Make it a family outing and have the children help you locate the plants along your walkout routes. Become personally able to identify these plants and make sure you know which ones are poisonous. You do not want to give the wrong herb to a loved one.

First aid kit—While prepackaged home first aid kits are convenient, they're usually way to bulky for a backpack. While a chemical ice pack or hot pack is nice to have, lugging them is additional weight. On the other hand, salt tablets, and a sterile eyewash kit are must-haves in any backpack first aid kit. This is why you need to make your own compact first aid kit based on your region, needs, and circumstances.

When choosing non-prescription items, favor light items that can keep you moving forward on your walkout. For example, pack pain medicine such as aspirin and naproxen, anti-diarrhea tablets, and activated charcoal tablets or capsules for poisoning. Do not forget about menstrual cramps. To save space, remove the medication from the bottles or boxes and place them into small, well-labeled zipper or sealable plastic bags. Also add sun block or zinc oxide (again make sure it is unscented to avoid attracting insects) and lip balm such as Carmex.

Blisters and splinters will slow you down, as will menstrual cramps. Make a small kit with practical things like small scissors, needles, tweezers, bandages, antibiotic cream, and strike-on-anything matches. Include a few sutures as well, to close serious wounds. You can use a Leatherman multi-tool as a crude needle driver. Add a small bag of fine ground cayenne pepper to use as a clotting agent on wounds (clean, white spider webs are also good to use as a clotting agent).

Last but not least, make sure you have a good first aid booklet to help you deal with various types of wounds, and help you know how to recognize and treat a person who is going into or who has already slipped into a state of shock. In any type of disaster, people will slip in and out of shock by means of very simple triggers such as a memory brought on by a joke, a song, scenery, a sunset or sunrise, a smell, and so forth. They my also suffer from the inability to accept what has happened. Be prepared—their life may depend on you recognizing the symptoms of shock.

Mouse or rat traps—Rodents are the most diverse species out there. All are edible and easy to catch. Gutted and skinned, they can be eaten uncooked after they have been sun dried into jerky. A mouse or rat trap is small and lightweight, and eating rodents is much better than starving!

Big black plastic garbage bags—Not only can this versatile item be used as a waterproof lining for your backpack, it can be cut down the sides and used as a moisture barrier when sleeping on the ground, part of a lean-to, as a windbreak, as a raincoat, or as a device to gather rainwater.

Clear plastic—Another very versatile item is a 10x10 foot sheet of clear plastic. It can be used in a similar manner as a black plastic bag and comes in handy in the construction of a water still.

Plastic tubing—Bring at least one 9-foot length (could be cut into three equal lengths) of plastic tubing for each backpack. This flexible straw can be used for anything from drinking water to a tourniquet.

Clothing Items

Whatever shoes and clothing you'll need will vary depending upon your own needs, plans, and geographical location, but always keep the following three suggestions in mind:

1. When you're outside, you're vulnerable to all forms of radiation, but you can mitigate the effect of UV radiation with the proper clothing.
2. A walkout is never the right time to break in anything new. Whatever clothing you're going to set aside for your walkout plan, wash it, wear it, test it, refine it, and test again. The same goes for shoes—break them in well before setting them aside.
3. Keep your walkout clothes and shoes clean and packed away in collapsible packaging, such as vacuum-packed space bags.

Comfort is important, so if you lose or gain weight, check items of your clothing, as well as your gear. To check them, take them out, inspect them, wear them, replace them as needed, and re-pack them.

With that in mind, consider the following clothing items:

Boots—No matter what else you do, this is where you've got to dig deep—pull out the money and buy a good pair of boots. To ensure the boots fit, bring along or wear a thick pair of socks or a pair of all-weather wool socks. Now you are ready to purchase good-fitting, high-top leather boots in which you can walk eight to ten miles a day. Get them from a trusted brand so you know they are well-stitched together (not glued) with top grain leather that will protect your ankles from minor twists and snakebites.

Never, never buy a pair of hiking boots from a discount store. If you buy a cheap pair of boots made for a fast turnover discount store, your feet will likely begin to hurt so badly during a long walkout, every step will become an excruciating act of agony. You are setting yourself up and placing your life in danger because unbeknown to you, you're walking in a fog of pain. This is when you will become oblivious to the dangers around you. Then you will find yourself with broken blisters, unable to travel further, placing unnecessary burdens upon your family, or even preventing your family from reaching their safe haven.

> **Note**—For those on a limited budget, you can usually find a pair of surplus military-spec combat boots at Army surplus stores, gun shows, or over the Internet. Shop around and get the best leather stitched boots you can afford. Then break them in by going on long hikes as you scout out the various walkout routes, rally points, and rest stops.

Hat—A good hat will be your most important piece of UV protection, so avoid breezy Panama hats and comfortable baseball caps. You will want a wide-brimmed hat with a solid fabric such as leather, heavy felt or canvas, depending upon your climate and preferences. Expect high winds due to abnormal weather, so consider the many variations of cowboy/Australian hats with a chinstrap.

Goggles—Losing your sight because of excessive UV radiation, ash, or pumice can be a death sentence. During low-wind periods, always wear a good pair of sport sunglasses with high-impact lenses and strong UV protection. If you wear prescription eyeglasses, you can also order prescription sunglasses with strong UV protection.

For protection from high winds and small wind projectiles, a high-impact military goggle with polycarbonate anti-fog lenses is best, but very expensive. Alternatively, you can keep an inexpensive pair of clear swim goggles with polycarbonate lenses and UV protection in your pack to protect your eyes from dust, smoke, volcanic pumice, ash, and sand.

Bandanna—Bandannas help control body heat, provide heat cover, and help keep flying pumice and dust out of the mouth or from slipping under the collar. Go for natural fabrics and bright colors that can be seen at a distance when waved over the head. Larger bandannas that are 40x40 inches can also be used as arm slings.

Clothes—Think twice before wearing cotton, because cotton-based material holds sweat and can freeze. Think modern—look for foul-weather gear and clothing made with synthetic fibers or a mix of various types of fiber, including wool, nylon, polyester, or leather, with a Gore-Tex lining. Remember: you are looking for clothing that will breath, that is light, and that can handle diverse weather conditions. If you are in a cold climate, you may want to wear only lama-wool long-sleeve shirts. You should also wear pants based on climate conditions, but the normal choice would be heavy-duty Carhartt work pants, military fatigues (preferably a solid green, not modern day camouflage fatigues so others will not assume you are a member of some kind of militia and shoot you), or khaki cargo pants. Your clothing needs to be loose-fitting and comfortable. A military uniform web belt is better than a leather belt, because it is more durable, and it can be easily adapted for other applications, such as a tourniquet.

Blue pants or shirts are highly visible to wildlife. This color stands out to animals like florescent orange does to humans, because blue is not a natural land color in the wild.

Leather jacket or vest—Leather is best because it acts like a second skin for your body and offers excellent protection from exposure, UV radiation, and abrasion. A leather jacket with a liner or a separate vest is recommended for those in cooler climates. For warmer climates, consider a light vest. Forget the style statements and go for the pockets and heavy stitching.

Change of socks and underwear—Survival can be a scary business, and after standing in dirty water to pull someone out of debris, a dry pair of socks is a nice thing to have. They also prevent the onset of blisters due to wet feet.

Store your socks and underwear in a sealable plastic bag, and keep an extra bag inside that so you have a clean bag and a soiled bag. If you soil yourself because you got diarrhea from something you ate or drank along the way, a fresh pair of underwear will help you feel somewhat normal again.

Insulated underwear—*Do not* buy cotton insulated underwear. Again, think synthetics. Look at insulated underwear for men and women that is made with silk. Silk provides the best wicking action and has one of the highest thermal ratings.

Leather work gloves—In the years to come, medical care is going to become strained, and the supply of antibiotics and painkillers we now take for granted will become scarce, if not completely exhausted. When you have to do something such as clearing brush or digging a fire pit, take a moment and put on a pair of sturdy work gloves. Remember, even a small cut can become a death sentence if infection sets in and you do not know of the proper herbal planets to use.

Heavy duty web belt—A heavy duty web belt, such as the kind used by construction workers, will help distribute part of the load from your back to your hips, making it easier to carry more.

Do not forget that all non-food items have long shelf lives, but should still be inspected periodically to make sure they are all in good shape, still fit, and are comfortable to wear. You do not want to find out that you have outgrown your clothing or boots while on the walkout, now do you?

Packing the Backpack

Your shopping spree is done and all of your survival stuff is lying on the floor before you. Now it is time to pack all that stuff, one-by-one, in the backpacks. Remember, as you pack all of it away, to stay within the weight limits of each person's capabilities.

To save you from first-time packing issues, pack clothes, socks and soft items against your back, and place the walking-snacks and toilet paper on top to prevent unnecessary unpacking and repacking. Here is a great concept to follow: Need should dictate accessibility—place the most used items on top.

Now it is time to weigh the backpacks. Make any necessary adjustments, and then go camping. Become comfortable with your backpacks by working out the problems today.

Water

Water is the number one priority for your survival plan. You can't live long without it, especially in hot areas where you lose water rapidly through perspiration. Even in cold areas, you need a minimum of 2 quarts (liters) of water each day to maintain internal efficiency, or dehydration will set in and major complications will follow.

Dehydration

More than 75 percent of your body is composed of water. Dehydration occurs when you lose more fluid than you take in and your body doesn't have enough water and other fluids to carry out its normal functions.

The common causes of dehydration are heat, cold, stress, and exertion; but do not forget intense bouts of diarrhea, vomiting, fever, or excessive sweating. Inadequate intake of water during hot weather or exercise also may deplete your body's water stores. Anyone may become dehydrated, but young children, older adults, and people with chronic illnesses are at a higher risk. Mild dehydration can cause symptoms such as weakness, dizziness, and fatigue. Severe dehydration is a life-threatening medical emergency, and a death sentence if it happens on your walkout.

You can usually reverse mild to moderate dehydration by increasing your intake of fluids, but severe cases need immediate medical treatment. The safest approach is to not become dehydrated in the first place. You can do that by monitoring your fluid loss during hot weather, illness, or exercise, and drinking enough liquids to replace what you lose.

Anyone can become dehydrated if the loss of fluids outweighs fluid intake, but certain people are at greater risk.

Infants and children—Worldwide, dehydration caused by diarrhea is the leading cause of death in children. Infants and children are especially vulnerable because of their relatively small body weights and high turnover of water and electrolytes. They are also the group most likely to experience diarrhea. In the United States, diarrhea remains one of the most common childhood illnesses.

Older adults—As you age, you become more susceptible to dehydration for several reasons: (1) your body's inability to conserve water, (2) your sense of thirst becomes less acute, and (3) it becomes harder for your body to respond to changes in temperature. What's more, older adults, especially during times of stress or a change in habits or environment, tend to eat less than younger people do and may sometimes forget to eat or drink altogether.

Another major concern is the older adult's physical condition. As seniors exert themselves, panting may occur due to not being accustomed to walking. Panting increases the amount of water needed, and if not taken into account and monitored, this simple body response could cause dehydration.

Signs of dehydration—The United States National Library of Medicine lists these common warning signs of significant dehydration:

- Not being able to urinate, or urinating very little.
- Urine that is very concentrated, has a dark yellow color, and may have a pungent/foul odor.
- Not being able to produce tears.
- Sunken eyes.
- In infants, the soft spot on the head is significantly sunken.
- Lethargy, dizziness, or lightheadedness.

Dehydration should not be ignored. During a normal lifestyle, if any of the signs of dehydration occurred, you would see a doctor immediately.

Complications from dehydration—Dehydration can lead to serious complications, including:

- *Heatstroke*—Inadequate fluid intake combined with vigorous exercise and heavy perspiration can lead to heat injury. Such injuries range in severity from mild heat cramps, to heat exhaustion, to potentially life-threatening heatstroke (discussed in detail in chapter 11).

- *Swelling of the brain (cerebral edema)*—Most often, the fluid you lose when you're dehydrated contains the same amount of sodium your blood does (isotonic dehydration). In some instances though, you may lose more sodium than fluid (hypotonic dehydration). To compensate for this loss, your body produces particles that pull water back into the cells. As a result, your cells may absorb too much water during the rehydration process, causing them to swell and rupture. The consequences are especially grave when brain cells are affected.
- *Seizures*—These occur when the normal electrical discharges in your brain become disorganized, leading to involuntary muscle contractions and sometimes to a loss of consciousness.
- *Hypovolemic shock*—This is one of the most serious complications of dehydration. It occurs when low blood volume causes a drop in blood pressure and a corresponding reduction in the amount of oxygen reaching your tissues. If untreated, severe hypovolemic shock can cause death in a matter of minutes.
- *Kidney failure*—This potentially life-threatening problem occurs when your kidneys are no longer able to remove excess fluids and waste from your blood.
- *Coma and death*—When not treated promptly and appropriately, severe dehydration can be fatal.

Treatment of dehydration—The only effective treatment for dehydration is to replace lost fluids. A physician should monitor this process, because your doctor can offer specific suggestions for treating dehydration. But some general guidelines include the following:

- *Oral rehydration solution*—Unless your doctor advises otherwise, use an oral rehydration solution such as Pedialyte for infants and children who have diarrhea, vomiting, or fever. These solutions contain water and salts in specific proportions to replenish both fluids and electrolytes. They also contain glucose or another carbohydrate such as rice powder to enhance absorption in the intestinal tract.
- *Making your own rehydration solution*—You can make your own oral rehydration solution by mixing ½ teaspoon salt, ½ teaspoon baking soda, 3 tablespoons sugar, and 1 liter of safe drinking water. Be sure to measure accurately because incorrect amounts can make the solution less effective or even harmful. If possible,

have someone else check your measurements for accuracy.

- *Treatment dosage*—A general rule of thumb is to keep giving liquids slowly until the person's urine becomes clear in color. If the person is vomiting, try giving small amounts of solution at frequent intervals—1 teaspoon every minute, for instance. If the person can't keep this down, wait thirty to sixty minutes and try again. Room temperature fluids are best.

Note—If the person is suffering with diarrhea, add a diuretic solution to their diet and continue giving them the rehydration solution until they recover from the diarrhea. Also monitor the person's food and drink to ensure the person is not complicating the problem by eating an unfamiliar food or drinking nonpotable water.

Preventing dehydration—To prevent dehydration, consume plenty of fluids, and foods high in water such as fruits and vegetables. According to the Institute of Medicine, letting thirst be your guide is an adequate daily guideline for most healthy people in normal circumstances. Fluids can be obtained not just from water but also from other beverages and foods. But on your walkout to your safe haven, you can't wait for thirst to alert you, you need to monitor water consumption to ensure that every person is drinking enough water each day. To function effectively, you must replace the fluid your body loses; therefore, your first goal is to obtain an adequate supply of water.

Water procurement is not as easy as you may think—all of the water on Earth is contaminated in one form or another and needs to be purified before you can drink it. To ensure your safety and that of your loved ones, never assume the water in a lake, pond, river, stream, or well is safe. Always purify your water before you drink it.

Water Sources

Almost every environment has some kind of water source present to some degree. How to locate it and determine if the water source is consumable is the next step. And the following will help you develop an understanding of how to find sources of water in various environments and how to make the water drinkable.

Frigid areas—Your main source of water will be snow and ice.

- *Snow and ice*—The first step is to gather the snow and ice, and then melt it. Remember to purify the water before you drink it; snow and ice are no more pure than the water from which they come. Do not eat snow or ice without melting it first! Eating snow and ice can reduce your body temperature and could possibly lead to more dehydration.

- *Sea ice*—Sea ice that is gray in color or opaque is salty. Do not use it without desalting it. Look for sea ice that is crystalline with a bluish cast because it has little salt in it.

Desert areas—There are numerous sources of water in a desert area.

- *Ground*—Your main source of water will be found in valley areas and low areas at the foot of concave banks, of dry river beds, at the foot of cliffs or rock outcrops, at the first depression behind the first sand dune of dry desert lakes, or wherever you find damp surface sand or green vegetation. To access this source of water, dig holes in the sand deep enough to allow water to seep in. In a sand dune belt, any available water will be found beneath the original valley floor at the edge of dunes. Utilize one of the filtration methods mentioned later in this chapter to help clear up the water, and then purify it.
- *Cacti*—Cut off the top of a barrel cactus and mash or squeeze the pulp. Do not eat pulp. Place the pulp in your mouth, suck out juice, and then spit out the pulp. This is where a machete or your 7-inch knife comes in handy. Cutting into a cactus is difficult and it takes time to get past the long, strong spines and cut through the tough rind.
- *Rocks*—Look for depressions, holes, and fissures in porous rocks. Periodic rainfall may collect in pools, seep into fissures, or collect in holes in rocks. To access this water, insert a flexible tube and siphon the water into a container, or use a piece of cloth to absorb the water and wring it out into a container. If a fissure is large enough, you can lower a container into it. Before you drink it, remember to purify the water—you do not know who might have been there before you.
- *Condensation*—We will discuss this in greater detail later in this chapter. No matter if you make a still to gather water or come across metal or plastic objects, use a piece of cloth to absorb the water and then wring the water from cloth into a container. The extreme temperature variations between night and day in the desert may cause condensation on metal and plastic surfaces.
- *Animal trails*—All trails lead to water. But which way do you go?

You should follow in the direction in which the trails converge. Signs of camps, campfire ashes, animal droppings, and trampled terrain may mark trails.

- *Birds*—Also watch for flocks of birds, as they will circle over water holes. Some birds fly to water holes at dawn and sunset. Their flight at these times is generally fast and close to the ground. Bird tracks or chirping sounds in the evening or early morning sometimes indicate that water is nearby. Bird droppings around a crack in the rocks may also indicate water in or near the crack.

If you do not have a reliable source to replenish your water supply, stay alert for ways in which your environment can help you.

Beach—Your main source of water will again be found in the ground. Start by digging a hole deep enough to allow water to seep in. While the hole is slowly filling with water, gather several rocks about the size of the hole and build a fire to heat the rocks. Once the rocks are hot, drop them in the water. Then hold a piece of cloth over the water hole to absorb the steam; wring the water from the cloth into a container. An alternate method is, if a container or bark pot is available, to fill the container or pot with sea water. Build a fire and boil the sea water to produce steam. Again hold a piece of cloth over the container to absorb the steam; wring the water from cloth into a container.

At sea—You could have several sources of water.

- *Sea water*—Always use a "desalting kit" or process. Never drink sea water without desalting.
- *Rain*—Catch the rain in a tarp or in other water-holding materials or containers. If the tarp or the water-holding material has become encrusted with salt, wash it in the sea before using.
- *Sea ice*—Please review this topic in the section on frigid areas.

Tropics—Water is abundant if you know where to look. Not only can you gather water during rainstorms, but you can gather it from various kinds of plants.

- *Green bamboo thickets*—These are an excellent source of fresh water. Water from green bamboo is clear and odorless. To get the water, bend a green bamboo stalk, tie it down, and cut off the top. The water will drip freely during the night. Old, cracked bamboo may also contain water.

- *Banana or plantain trees*—Wherever you find banana or plantain trees, you can get water. Cut down the tree, leaving about a 12-inch (30-centimeter) stump, and scoop out the center of the stump so that the hollow is bowl-shaped. Water from the roots will immediately start to fill the hollow. The first three fillings of water will be bitter, but the following fillings will be palatable. The stump will supply water for up to four days. Be sure keep it covered, to keep insects out.
- *Tropical vines*—Some tropical vines can give you water. Cut a notch in the vine as high as you can reach, then cut the vine off close to the ground. Catch the dropping liquid in a container or in your mouth.

Warning—Do not drink the liquid from a tropical vine if it is sticky, milky, or bitter tasting.

- *Coconuts*—The milk from a green (unripe) coconut is a good thirst quencher; however, the milk from a mature coconut contains oil that acts as a laxative. Always drink a new source of fluid in moderation until your body becomes accustom.

Other sources of water—Be open-minded in your search for water. Here are a few more ideas to get your imagination flowing:

- *Dew*—Heavy dew can provide water. Tie rags or tufts of fine grass around your ankles and walk through dew-covered grass before sunrise. As the rags or grass tufts absorb the dew, wring the water into a container. Repeat the process until you have a supply of water or until the dew is gone. In Australia, the Aborigines have been known to mop up as much as a liter an hour this way.
- *Insects*—Bees or ants going into a hole in a tree may point to a water-filled hole. Siphon the water with plastic tubing or scoop it up with an improvised dipper. You can also stuff cloth in the hole to absorb the water and then wring it from the cloth.
- *Plants*—In the American tropics you may find large trees whose branches support air plants. These air plants may hold a considerable amount of rainwater in their overlapping, thickly growing leaves. Strain the water through a cloth to remove insects and debris.
- *Pulpy centers*—You can get water from plants with moist pulpy centers. Cut off a section of the plant and squeeze or smash

the pulp so that the moisture runs out. Catch the liquid in a container.

- *Roots*—Plant roots may provide water. Dig or pry the roots out of the ground, cut them into short pieces, and smash the pulp so the moisture runs out. Catch the liquid in a container.
- *Leaves*—Fleshy leaves, stems, or stalks such as bamboo contain water. Cut or notch the stalks at the base of a joint to drain out the liquid.

Warning—Do not drink the liquid from a plant if it is sticky, milky, or bitter tasting.

Trees—Besides rock crevices, water sometimes gathers in tree crotches. Use the above procedures to get the water. The following trees can also provide water:

- *Palms*—Palms, such as the buri, coconut, sugar, rattan, and nips, contain liquid. Bruise a lower frond and pull it down so the tree will "bleed" at the injury.
- *Traveler's tree*—This tree has a cup-like sheath at the base of its leaves in which water collects.
- *Umbrella tree*—The leaf bases and roots of this tropical tree can provide water.
- *Baobab tree*—This tree of the sandy plains collects water in its bottle-like trunk during the wet season. Frequently, you can find clear, fresh water in these trees after weeks of dry weather.

Word of caution pertaining to tree sap—Do not keep the sap from plants longer than 24 hours. It begins fermenting and becomes a dangerous water source.

Do not use the following—No matter what, do not replace your daily water needs with the following:

- *Alcohol*—Alcoholic beverages dehydrate the body and cloud judgment.
- *Urine*—Urine contains harmful body waste and about 2 percent salt.
- *Blood*—Animal and even human blood is salty and is considered a food by your body; therefore, it requires additional body fluids to digest. Blood may also transmit disease.
- *Sea water*—Sea water or ocean water, is about 4 percent salt. It takes about two quarts (liters) of body fluids to rid the body of

waste from one quart (liter) of sea water. Therefore, by drinking sea water you deplete your body's water supply, which can cause death. Don't do it! It's not worth the risk.

Water Stills

You can use water stills in various climates and areas of the world to collect water. These stills can be built to draw moisture from plant material and from the ground. This is where the plastic bags and the plastic tubing come in handy. It also takes time and patience to let the still collect the water. How much time you might ask? It takes about 24 hours to get one-half to 1 quart (liter) of water.

You also need to take into account is the amount of water each still generates and the minimum needs of each person in your group. Since it takes 24 hours to collect between ½ to 1 quart of water, and each person needs a minimum of 2 quarts per day, it will take at least 3 stills to meet one person's daily water intake needs.

Do not become down-hearted. Instead, take this in stride and plan ahead. Use the water stills to gather water during the evening, overnight and early morning, then supplement your water needs through other sources during the day. Be flexible. Be open-minded and resourceful, ever alert to what the geographical environment is offering.

Aboveground still—To make the aboveground still, you need a sunny slope on which to place the still, a clear plastic bag, green leafy vegetation, and a small rock. (See Figure 6-1.)

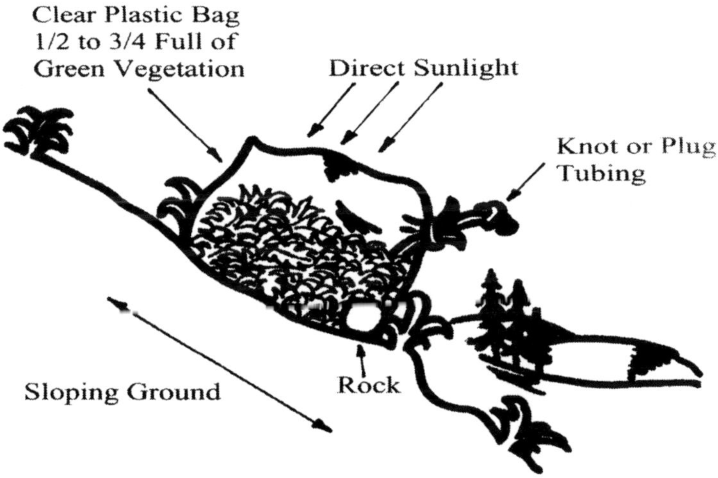

Figure 6 - 1 Aboveground Solar Water Still

To make the aboveground still—After gathering up the needed material, utilize the following steps to make your aboveground water still:

1. Fill the bag with air by turning the opening into the breeze or by popping the bag in the air.
2. Fill the plastic bag ½ to ¾ full of green leafy vegetation.* Be sure to remove all hard sticks or sharp spines that might puncture the bag.

*__Warning__—*Do not* use poisonous plants, because it will produce a poisonous liquid!

3. Place a small rock or similar item in the bag.
4. Close the bag and tie the mouth securely as close to the end of the bag as possible to keep the maximum amount of air space. If you have a piece of tubing, a small straw, or a hollow reed, insert one end in the mouth of the bag before you tie it securely. Then tie off or plug the tubing so that air will not escape. This tubing will allow you to drain out condensed water without untying the bag.
5. Place the bag, mouth downhill, on a slope in full sunlight. Position the mouth of the bag slightly higher than the low point in the bag.
6. Settle the bag in place so that the rock works itself into the low point in the bag.

To get the condensed water from the still, loosen the tie around the bag's mouth and tip the bag so that the water collected around the rock will drain out. Then re-tie the mouth securely and reposition the still to allow further condensation.

Change the vegetation in the bag after extracting most of the water from it. This will ensure maximum output of water.

Belowground still—To make a belowground still, you need a digging tool, a container, a plastic sheet, a drinking tube, and a rock. (See Figure 6-2.)

Select a site where you believe the soil will contain moisture (such as a dry stream bed or a low spot where rainwater has collected). The soil at this site should be easy to dig, and sunlight must hit the site most of the day. To construct the still, gather the necessary materials and follow the steps on the following page.

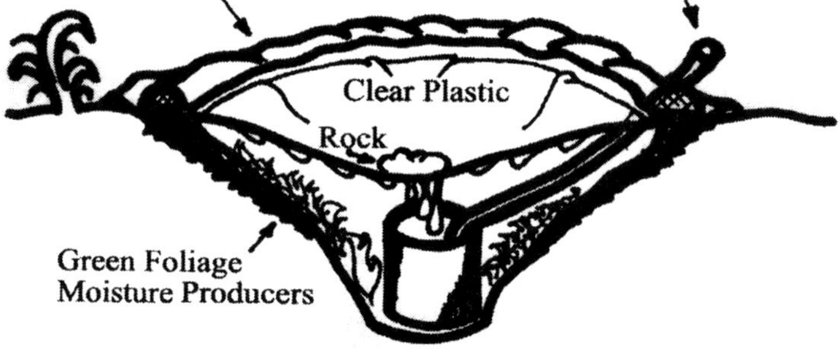

Figure 6 - 2 Belowground Still

To make the belowground still—

1. Dig a bowl-shaped hole about 3 feet (1 meter) across and 2 feet (60 centimeters) deep.
2. Dig a sump in the center of the hole. The sump's depth and perimeter will depend on the size of the container that you have to place in it. The bottom of the sump should allow the container to stand upright.
3. Anchor the tubing to the container's bottom by forming a loose overhand knot in the tubing.
4. Place the container upright in the sump.
5. Extend the unanchored end of the tubing up, over, and beyond the lip of the hole.
6. Place the plastic sheet over the hole, covering its edges with soil to hold it in place.
7. Place a rock in the center of the plastic sheet.
8. Lower the plastic sheet into the hole until it is about 12 to 16 inches (30 to 40 centimeters) below ground level. It now forms an inverted cone with the rock at its apex. Make sure that the cone's apex is directly over your container. Also make sure the plastic cone does not touch the sides of the hole because the earth will absorb the condensed water.
9. Put more soil on the edges of the plastic to hold it securely in place and to prevent the loss of moisture.

10. Plug the tube when not in use so that the moisture will not evaporate.

You can drink water without disturbing the still by using the tube as a straw. You may want to use plants in the hole as a moisture source. If so, dig out additional soil from the sides of the hole to form a slope on which to place the plants. Then proceed as outlined above.

Belowground still for use with polluted water—If polluted water is your only moisture source, dig a small trough outside the hole about 10 inches (25 centimeters) from the still's lip. (See Figure 6-3.) Dig the trough about 10 inches (25 centimeters) deep and 4 inches (8 centimeters) wide. Pour the polluted water in the trough. Be sure you do not spill any polluted water around the rim of the hole where the plastic sheet touches the soil. The trough holds the polluted water and the soil filters it as the still draws it in. The water then condenses on the plastic and drains into the container.

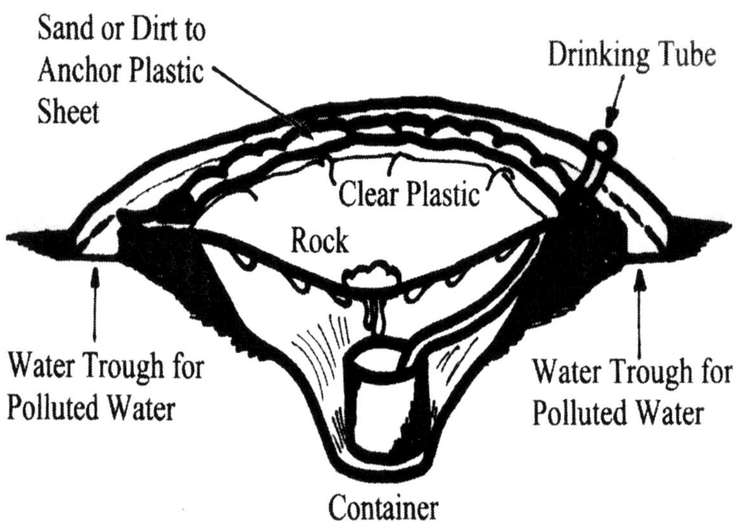

Figure 6 - 3 Belowground Still when using Polluted Water

Belowground still for use with saltwater—Utilize the same procedures you used with the belowground still for use with polluted water. Only this time pour saltwater into the trough.

Water Purification

During your walkout to your safe haven, always take the time to purify the water. Do not take the chance of placing the health and well-being of yourself or your loved ones in danger by assuming any water source is safe to drink because it looks clear and clean. Rainwater, if collected in clean containers or in plants free of insects or debris, is usually safe for drinking. However, you need to purify water from lakes, ponds, swamps, springs, or streams—especially the water near human settlements or in the tropics.

When possible, purify all the water you got from vegetation or from the ground by using any of the following water purification methods:

Boiling water—One of the best methods for treating water is the boiling method. Here is a simple rule of thumb to follow: Boil water for one minute at sea level, adding one minute for each additional 1000 feet (300 meters) above sea level, or boil for ten minutes no matter where you are to produce germ-free water for drinking or cooking. Since boiling leaves water with a flat taste, you should pour it back and forth between two containers several times once it has cooled. This aerates the water, restoring its natural taste. A vessel for boiling water can be formed from the aluminum foil in your survival kit.

Halazone tablets—Drugstores, sporting goods stores, and outfitter stores usually have Halazone tablets or Potable Aqua tablets for the treatment of water. Halazone tablets have been used successfully for years. Add two tablets to a 32-ounce bottle of water and wait for 30 minutes before drinking.

Potable aqua tablets—The newer product, Potable Aqua, requires one tablet to every 32 ounces of water. Cap loosely to allow a little leakage cause by the fizzing reaction. Wait 3 minutes and shake thoroughly. Wait another 10 minutes before drinking. If the water is very cold or contains rotten leaves or silt, use 2 tablets and wait 20 minutes before drinking.

Bleach treatment—Bleach is another excellent water treatment. To use this process, the first step is to locate a bottle with a dropper, and then fill it with bleach. The amount you want to use is 2 drops of bleach to a 32-ounce container (quart) of water. If the water source is cloudy, add 4 drops. Then shake the water vigorously and let it sit for 30 minutes. There should be a slight chlorine odor and taste if the water is properly treated. If not, add another 2 drops of bleach and let the water stand for an additional 15 minutes.

Iodine and betadine treatment—While iodine is no longer used in some of the newer first-aid kits, it is still in older kits and makes a good water treatment. Before using, ensure no one is allergic to iodine, because an allergic reaction to iodine may result in death.

Today, over-the-counter iodine is 2 percent Tincture of Iodine or 10 percent Betadine solution. You can also use both of these for first aid.

For a 32-ounce container, you can use eight drops of 2 percent Tincture of Iodine or four drops of Betadine solution to disinfect the water. Allow the water to sit for thirty minutes for clear water and sixty minutes for cloudy water.

Microfilter or microbiological water filter pump—These pumps come in various sizes and weights. Shop around and find the one best suited for you and your family. One step to help you determine which one is best for you is how many gallons of water the filter will process. On average, most small pump filters will process 200 gallons of water before the filter will need to be cleaned and/or changed. Another is the type of filter. This filter system removes all microorganisms larger than one micron. There are other filter systems that will also remove smaller viruses, and they cost a lot more.

Purify, purify, and purify before you drink. Always have more than one source to purify the water, or this could happen to you:

> In June of 2008, my friend (home on leave from the Army) and I decided to go camping for a couple of days in the beautiful mountains of Wyoming. We talked about all the things we needed and worked to keep each backpack around thirty pounds. Since I had my trusty water filter pump, we left all other commercial sources of purification at the house. The walk into the mountains was wonderful. Everything was green, the wild flowers were blooming, deer and elk were out enjoying the new lush green sprouts of grass, and a bouquet of scents and smells of springtime perfumed the soft mountain breeze. When we arrived at our destination, I immediately filled our canteens and went about setting up camp. After draining my canteen again, I returned to the mountain stream that flowed behind our camp and experienced a rude awakening—my water filter pump would not work. Instead of exploring the countryside as planned, we spent the next two days wasting our free time, maintaining a fire so we could boil water, one quart at a time.

Never assume. Make the space in your backpack for as many water purification devices as possible. That way you will always be prepared for the unexpected. In the end, the best way to purify water is to boil it. And if you are squeamish about the color or cloudy look of the boiled water, then filter the water to remove the debris and bodies of dead waterborne parasites.

Water Filtration Devices

If the only water you can locate is muddy, stagnant, and foul smelling, you can clear the water several different ways:

Standing method—Collect the water in a container and let it stand for 12 hours. Then scoop the clear water into another container, or carefully pour it into another container without stirring up the settlement.

Filtration method—Pour the water through a filtering system.

To make a filtering system, place several inches (centimeters) or layers of filtering material such as sand, crushed rock, charcoal, or cloth in bamboo, a hollow log, or an article of clothing. (See Figure 6-4.) And remember to place a container underneath to catch the filtered water.

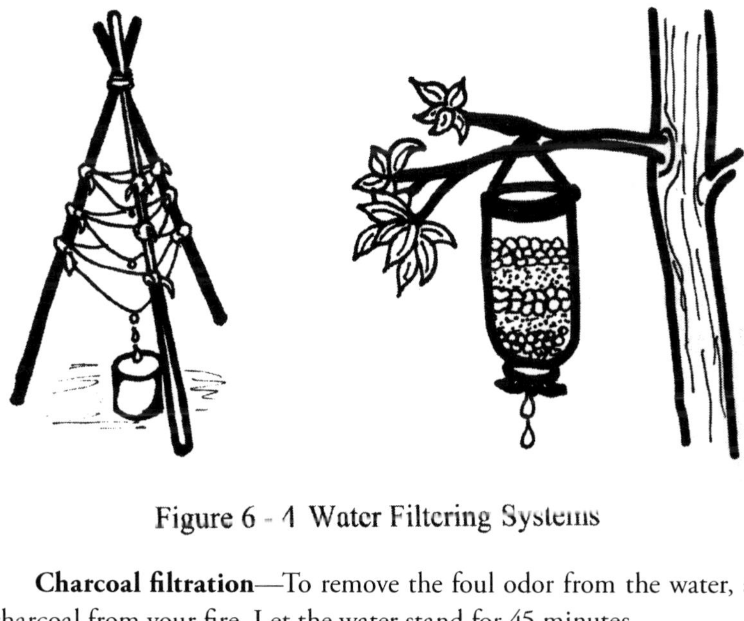

Figure 6 - 4 Water Filtering Systems

Charcoal filtration—To remove the foul odor from the water, add charcoal from your fire. Let the water stand for 45 minutes.

Note—These filtering procedures only clear the water and make it more palatable. You will still have to purify the water before drinking it.

Why the Need to Purify the Water

In recent studies released by the Department of Health, all water sources in North America are contaminated and have been declared unhealthy for human consumption without first being purified. The study also advised that all water sources on the earth are polluted in one form or another. Do not be misled by TV commercials that depict clear mountain streams as being safe to drink—clear water is not a sign for safe consumption.

If you should find yourself in a situation where you and your loved ones have gone for a couple of days without water, and finally find a water source, please take the time to purify it before drinking to prevent exposure to diseases and swallowing organisms that can harm you. Here are a few examples of many diseases and organisms living in the water that can cause illnesses or even death:

Dysentery—Symptoms of dysentery include severe diarrhea with bloody stools, fever, and weakness. The primary cause of dysentery is called "crytosporidium," or waterborne parasites. These parasites will kill if left untreated. Human, animal, and insect feces in the water cause another form of dysentery. The simplest step to prevent you from coming down with dysentery is to purify the water. Dysentery is not something you want to deal with on a walkout.

Cholera and typhoid—You may be susceptible to these diseases regardless of inoculations.

Flukes—Stagnant, polluted water—especially in tropical areas—often contains blood flukes. If you swallow flukes, they will bore into the bloodstream, live as parasites, and cause disease.

Leeches—If you swallow a leech, it can hook onto the throat passage or inside the nose. It will suck blood, create a wound, and move to another area. Each bleeding wound may become infected.

All of these, if untreated, will lead to death. Remember that you and your loved ones are not alone as you travel to your safe haven. There could be millions of people out there doing the same. And some of those people may intentionally, or unintentionally do nasty things to the water.

Shelter

The second priority on your survival list is shelter. A shelter can protect you and your loved ones from the sun, insects, wind, rain, snow, hot or cold temperatures, hypothermia, and unwanted observation. It can give your family a feeling of well-being. It can help you maintain your will to survive—no matter how bad it may seem at the time.

There may come a time where your need for shelter may take precedence over your need for food or even water. For example, prolonged exposure to a cold, frigid area can cause excessive fatigue and weakness (exhaustion). An exhausted person may develop a passive outlook, thereby losing the will to survive, and placing everyone in dangerous of the effects of hypothermia.

Hypothermia

Hypothermia, in several circles of medical research, is considered more dangerous than dehydration. In other circles of research, dehydration and hypothermia go hand-in-hand, but I think the best definition come from the Boy Scout's Manual, "long lasting chill, can kill." No matter how you look at it, in a survival situation, you must take care of yourself in order to protect your loved ones. Therefore, the first step in the process is to understand hypothermia.

Hypothermia is the lowering of the core temperature of the body. It can strike in any season and in almost any climate. All that is needed is a mild air temperature—30 to 70 degrees Fahrenheit—wetness, rain, sweat, a creek dunking, a slight wind, and a tired person.

Hypothermia attacks a person in two steps. The first is when your body begins to lose heat faster than it produces it. At this point, you are aware of feeling cold, and the shivers begin.

The second step is when the cold reaches the brain, depriving you of good judgment. It is at this point that confusion will take over decision-making. This is the reason almost no one recognizes that he or she has hypothermia. In the second stage, your internal temperature slides downward. Without treatment, this slide leads to stupor, collapse, and death. Each year many people become lost due to confusion brought on by early stages of hypothermia.

Ways to Avoid Hypothermia

Stay dry—When clothing gets wet it may lose 90 percent of its insulation value (discussed in detail in chapter 11). Even sweating can bring on hypothermia. That is why in cold weather, it is better to stay away from clothing made of cotton, for it retains body sweat—think wool, silk, and synthetics.

Beware of wind chill—A slight breeze carries heat away from bare skin faster than still air. It turns wet cloths into a refrigerator due to evaporation.

Understand cold—Most hypothermia cases develop in air temperatures that are considered mild, such as wind chill temperatures in the 30s through the 60s while the temperature gage reads in the 50s through the 70s. Most people do not believe such temperatures can be dangerous.

Terminate exposure—When you cannot stay warm and dry in existing weather conditions, either get a fire going at a natural shelter (discussed later in this chapter) out of the wind, or set up your tube tent and get into your sleeping bag. Get out of the wind and dampness and get warm as fast as you can.

Never ignore shivering—Persistent or violent shivering is clear warning that you are in early stages of hypothermia.

When hypothermia symptoms are noticed, treatment should begin immediately. First get the victim out of the weather and remove his wet clothing. If the victim is only mildly impaired, give him warm drinks, get him into dry clothing, and get him into a tube tent and a sleeping bag.

If the victim is semiconscious or worse, he does not have the capacity of regaining his body temperature without outside help. Keep him awake, give him warm drinks and, if possible, get him into a warm bath. If that's not possible, strip the victim and put him into a sleeping bag with another person. Skin-to-skin contact is an effective treatment.

As the body core temperature drops, here is how hypothermia will affect you:

- 98.6–96 degrees—You will experience uncontrolled shivering and your ability to perform complex tasks will be impaired.
- 95–91 degrees—You will experience violent shivering and difficulty speaking.
- 90–86 degrees—Your shivering decreases, muscles begin to stiffen, and you will lose coordination. Your mind becomes dull and in some cases, amnesia occurs.
- 85–81 degrees—You will become irrational and may drift into a stupor. Your pulse and respiration will slow. Your muscular rigidity continues.
- 80–78 degrees—You lapse into unconsciousness. Your reflexes cease to function and your heartbeat becomes erratic.
- Below 78 degrees—At this stage you will experience total failure of cardiac and respiration system. Death occurs.

In a survival situation, every effort should be made to avoid hypothermia. That means getting a warm camp set up before you get wet and cold. Don't put off getting a survival camp established. Delay can be deadly. For that reason, allow time before sunset to make a shelter.

Predicting the Time Before Sunset

Be nice to yourself and allow ample time before sunset to build your shelter, set up camp, and cook supper. At first, while you are still adjusting to your daily survival routine, give yourself at least two hours before sunset to find a suitable campsite. Here is a good way to predict the time you have left before sunset:

1. Face the horizon where the sun will set.
2. Extend both arms in front of you and make fists.
3. Place your right fist so it looks like it is resting on the horizon.* Now stack your left fist on your right. Count, as you continue to stack one fist on top of the other, how many fists are between the horizon and the sun.
4. Now multiply the number of fists counted by 25 minutes. A good rule to follow for both male and female adults is 5 fists equals 2 hours until sunset.

*Note—The tops of forests (or tree lines), hills, mountains to the west, is the horizon.

When it is time to stop for the night, be careful. Have everyone in the group take a break and, if possible, have everyone sit quietly so you can:

1. *Stop.* Close your eyes and listen. Ensure you are alone.
2. *Sit still.* Give it time to allow the animals and birds to resume their normal activity. Animal and bird noise is good.
3. *Observe.* Have a group member take a position where he can oversee the campsite and the area around. Taking extra precaution can save lives.

Now it is time to construct camp.

Constructing a Shelter

The most common error in making a shelter is to make it too large. A shelter must be large enough to protect you and yours. It must also be small enough to contain body heat—especially in cold climates.

A good definition for a camp or shelter is a "place affording protection from the elements." Every survivalist faced with the problem of protecting himself from the elements must consider using every conceivable place already existing in his immediate area, or using every available material at hand to improvise a place that will afford much-needed protection. When deciding what type of shelter to build, you must first consider what the shelter needs to protect you from, like rain, snow, cold, insects, and heat. As an example, when in hot, arid areas, protection from the sun during the day may be the prime consideration. In frigid areas, extreme cold aggravated by high winds, or in some seasons, swarms of insects may be the danger that dictates what type of protection you must seek.

In addition to protection from the natural elements and conditions, an adequate shelter will also provide you a reassuring feeling of psychological well-being that is so necessary for sound rest. Adequate rest is extremely important during your walkout to ensure your ability to make sound decisions. The need for rest becomes more critical as time passes and daily stresses of the walkout wears on you and your family. Rest contributes to mental and physical health, and adequate shelter contributes to sound rest. Because of these factors, adequate shelter must be placed high on your priority list for the survival of your family to be successful.

Constructing a good shelter where you and yours can rest comfortably out of the elements takes time and some work. So make it a family project because it will help keep your minds off your troubles.

The location of your shelter site will depend on several things. The first priority is to build your shelter in a place where passersby cannot easily see it. Avoid constructing your shelter in a low swap area or in a dry creek bed. The daily stress of your walkout is bad enough without getting caught in a flash flood or rising ground water. Take it from me: it is not fun to wake up and finding your self lying in three inches of water.

Another very important thing for you to do before building your shelter is to look up. Don't build your shelter under standing dead trees, dead limbs, branches heavy with snow, or below a steep slope. Always avoid avalanche-prone slopes. You don't want these things to fall on you. At the same time, do seek thick overhead vegetation that could assist in blocking the views of passersby. With the following precautions observed, you are ready to start the process of constructing a shelter where you can sleep comfortably. The next step is to select a level or a near-level site. Remove stones and sticks. Your sleep is vital to conserve energy for survival.

How effective your shelter will be depends upon what you have to construct it with and what the weather is like, plus your ability to improvise and any previous experience you have had in shelter construction. Now is the time to go camping and practice, practice, practice!

Types of Shelters

Tube tent—The tube tent is easy and quick to set up. You simply run a rope or cord through the plastic tube and tie it between two trees. Since they blow like a sail in high winds, it is a good idea to weigh down the front and rear openings with rocks or heavy logs.

Lean-to—A tarp, a poncho, any type of plastic (your garbage bags cut open), or even a space blanket makes an extremely versatile shelter. A rainproof lean-to is good in cold weather because when used with a reflector fire, the shelter can be comfortable in the worst weather. (See Figure 7-1 below.) Another example of a lean-to is Figure 8-1, in chapter 8.

The MPI space blanket, which is sold in many camping or sporting goods stores, is a good item to carry in your backpack. This blanket is made from a very thin, strong space-age material that can reflect 90 percent of the heat thrown against it. It is compact, about the size of a pack of cigarettes. It can be made into a lean-to and is very warm when used as a reflector fire. This blanket makes a warm sleeping bag when folded properly; therefore, include two or three in each pack.

Figure 7 - 1 Poncho Style Lean - to

To make the lean-to—gather up the needed materials and utilize the following steps:

1. If you are using a poncho, tie off the hood of the poncho. Pull the drawstring tight, roll the hood long ways, fold it into thirds, and tie it off with the drawstring.
2. Lay out the tarp, poncho, plastic sheet, or space blanket between the two trees. Measure how much rope you will need to tie the ends of the tarp to the trees. Cut the rope or parachute cord and remember to give yourself a little extra. On one long side of the tarp, tie half of the rope to the corner grommet. Tie the other half to the other corner grommet.
3. Attach a drip stick (about an 8-inch long stick) to each rope about 2½ inches from the grommet. These drip sticks will keep rainwater from running down the ropes into the lean-to. Tying strings (about 2–3 inches long) to each grommet along the tarp's top edge will allow the water to run to and down the line without dripping into the shelter.
4. Tie the ropes about waist high on the trees (uprights). It is best to use a quick-release knot.
5. Spread the tarp and anchor it to the ground, putting sharpened sticks through the grommets and into the ground.
6. If you plan to use the lean-to for more than one night, or you

expect rain, make a center support for the lean-to. If you are using a tarp or a space blanket, utilize a blunted-end stick that is several inches longer than the height of the tarp at the middle point between the waist-height top and the ground. Place the stick in the inside middle of the tarp. If you are using a poncho, make this support with a line. Attach one end of the line to the poncho hood and the other end to an overhanging branch. Make sure there is no slack in the line.

7. For additional protection from wind and rain, place some brush, your backpack, or other equipment at the sides of the lean-to.
8. To reduce heat loss to the ground, place some type of insulating material, such as leaves or pine needles, inside your lean-to.

Note—When lying on the ground, you lose as much as 80 percent of your body heat to the ground.

To increase your security from unwanted observation, lower the lean-to's silhouette by making two changes. First, secure the support lines to the trees at knee height (not at waist height) using two knee-high sticks in the two center grommets (sides of lean-to). Second, angle the tarp to the ground, securing it with sharpened sticks, as above.

Natural shelter—A rock overhang or cave makes one of the best natural shelters to be found. By building up rock or log walls as windbreaks, these shelters can actually be comfortable not only for you, but other creatures. Before moving in, be vigilant. Scorpions, spiders, snakes, rodents, and a host of nocturnal predators love rock overhangs. Examine the area closely in daylight before settling in for the night.

Many times, freshly blown-down trees can be made into a survival shelter by cutting away the limbs near the ground. If larger pieces of bark are around, use it to improve the roof. It would resemble something like the debris hut pictured below. (See Figure 7-2.)

Another natural shelter is a weeping spruce—a pine tree with drooping limbs. As you climb in, cut away only the limbs needed to make a cozy place to rest from the elements around. Save all the dry pinecones you find, they will come in handy when you start your fire. Remember fire safety: to start a fire under a tree could create a bigger fire. If you need to place the fire under the tree, trim the inner limbs at least four feet from the ground and keep your fire small, at the same time the smoke from the fire will be defused as it passes up through the weepy pine.

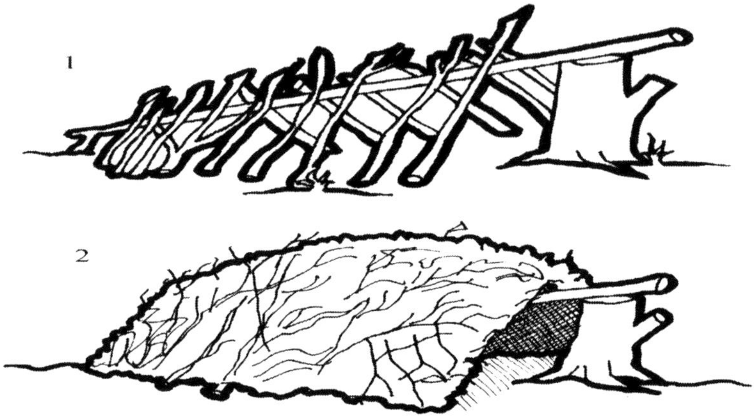

Figure 7 - 2 Debris Hut

Snow shelters—In the winter, there are several survival shelters that can be constructed. However, shelters such as the famous snow cave take a lot of energy and skill. The hole-in-the-snow shelter is one of the simpler shelters if the snow is at least 4 feet deep.

Hole-in-the-snow shelter—Find an evergreen tree that has limbs extending down to snow level, then dig out all the snow around its trunk right down to the ground. Next, trim all the inside branches and use them to line the bottom and finish the top. (See Figure 7-3.) You now have a very comfortable, hidden shelter.

Figure 7 - 3 Hole-in-the-snow Shelter

Snow cave—A snow cave is an excellent cold weather shelter, but it requires a lot of energy, a shovel or similar device, and some skill. Begin by finding a packed snowdrift that is 7 feet high and 12 feet or more wide. Then start digging a low tunnel into the snow bank. After you dig the tunnel 2 feet into the bank, hollow out an opening large enough for you to lie down.

Next, push a stick through the roof at a 45-degree angle to make a vent hole. In the back of the cave, build the bed platform at least 18 inches high. To conserve heat, the cave should be built just large enough to sleep, get dressed, and undress while lying in the sleeping bag. If desired, the sleeping shelf may be walled in to conserve heat. In addition to the ventilation hole through the roof, there should be another at the door if you push snow into the opening to block the outside elements. And remember, life in snow shelters is rugged, with temperatures reaching a few degrees above freezing.

This form of shelter is not one I would recommend—if not done correctly, you may be digging your own snow-grave.

Swamp bed—If you have to deal with a marsh or swamp, or any area with standing water or continually wet ground, the swamp bed keeps you out of the water. (See Figure 7-4.) When selecting such a site, consider the weather, wind, tides, and available materials.

Figure 7 - 4 Swamp Bed

To make a swamp bed, employ the following steps:

1. Look for four trees clustered in a rectangle or cut four poles (bamboo is ideal) and drive them firmly into the ground so they form a rectangle. They should be far enough apart and strong enough to support your height, weight, and your backpack.
2. Cut two poles that span the width of the rectangle. They, too, must be strong enough to support your weight.
3. Secure these two poles to the trees (or poles). Be sure they are high enough above the ground or water to allow for tides, high water, snakes and other nocturnal animals (believe me, it is a real surprise to have an unexpected creature crawl into bed with you).
4. Cut additional poles that span the rectangle's length. Lay them across the two side poles, and secure them.
5. Cover the top of the bed frame with broad leaves or grass to form a soft sleeping surface.
6. Build a fire pad by laying clay, silt, or mud on one corner of the swamp bed and allow it to dry.

Another shelter designed to get you above and out of the water or wet ground uses the same rectangular configuration as the swamp bed. You simply lay sticks and branches lengthwise on the inside of the trees (or poles) until there is enough material to raise the sleeping surface above the water level.

Desert shelter—In an arid environment, consider the time, effort, and material needed to make a shelter (cold at night, scorching during the day, and moisture gathers on everything just after sunrise). If you have material such as a tarp, poncho, a space blanket or other material, use it along with such terrain features as rock outcropping, mounds of sand, or a depression between dunes or rocks to make your shelter.

- **Using rock outcrops:**
  1. Anchor one end of your tarp (poncho, space blanket or other material) on the edge of the outcrop using rocks or other weights.
  2. Extend and anchor the other end of the poncho so it provides the best possible shade.
- **In a sandy area:**
  1. Build a mound of sand or use the side of a sand dune for one side of the shelter.

2. Anchor one end of the material on top of the mound using sand or other weights.
3. Extend and anchor the other end of the material so it provides the best possible shade.
4. To further reduce the temperature under the tarp, dig out a foot or so of sand and place it around the two sides of your tarp as additional insulation from the heat.

Note—If you have enough material, fold the tarp in half and create a 1 to 1.5 foot (30 to 45 centimeter) airspace between the two halves. This airspace will reduce the temperature under the shelter.

Be watchful for snakes and scorpions seeking a cool place out of the sun during the day, and a warm place to rest at night.

Solar storm shelter—Shielding yourself from the witch's brew of a solar storm requires the same level of preparation we already use when expecting tornadoes or severe storms. Remember reading in chapter 4 what the difference in dealing with a Solar Storm is—we look for a safe place where there is enough mass between us and what is trying to kill us.

The table below (from the American Physical Society online archive) starts with the minimum acceptable half-value thickness, a good value of thickness and the excellent thickness of common construction materials

	Half value (HV)	Good value (3 x HV)	Great value (7 x HV)
Material	**Inches/MM**	**Inches/MM**	**Inches/MM**
Copper	.5/12	1.5/36	3.5/84
Iron or Steel	.7/18	2.1/54	4.9/126
Brick	2/51	6/152	14/357
Concrete	2.2/56	6.6/168	15.4/392
Dirt	3.3/84	9.9/252	23.1/588
Ice	6.8/173	20.4/519	47.6/1211
Soft Wood	8.8/224	26.4/674	61.6/1568
Snow	20.3/516	60.9/1548	142.1/3612

you need to achieve a safe retreat from incoming gamma radiation.

During your walkout to your safe haven, to achieve a safe value/thickness of construction material, you may need to combine several different materials, to include natural shelter (dirt/rock) along with wood, metal (car hood, roofing tin, etc.), even snow. Keep calm and think.

There are many variations of shelters that can be made to protect us from all possibilities. The secret to shelter construction is simple—use what is available to protect you and your loved ones from the elements. Construct whatever shelter uses the least amount of energy to build. In most cases, the tube tent you carry in your backpack will be the best shelter for the family while you construct another from whatever is available around you. And again, while you have the time, go camping and practice, practice, practice.

Sleeping Warmly

Sleeping warmly and comfortably cannot be emphasized enough in a survival situation. You and your family need a lot of energy for the tasks ahead of you. You need to be thinking clearer and sharper than you do during your normal life, because the decisions you make will determine your well-being and the safe arrival at your walkout destination.

If you have a tube tent and a space blanket or bag in your pack, get the tube tent up so that you and yours can get into the bag before any of you get wet, then the chances are good that all of you will sleep warmly. How well you clean the tube tent site will determine how comfortable you sleep. Taking a few minutes to remove stones, sticks, and so forth, and laying down a bed of dry leaves can make the difference between a long miserable night and a comfortable, warm night of sleep.

What about a night spent without the aid of a tube tent, or a space blanket or sleeping bag? In this case, there are several options depending upon the terrain where you determine a camp. The first rule is to get into a shelter of some type that gives you protection from the rain, snow, volcanic ash, solar storm, or wind. If this shelter makes it easier for you to get a fire going, all the better. Your chances of actually getting some sleep improve when you can stay warm. Be sure to gather three times as much wood as you think you'll need, as it will probably take that much to keep the fire going all night. It is difficult to keep the body warm or to get enough sleep when you must make two or three trips out into the cold darkness to gather wood.

The ideal sleeping shelter, aside from the tube tent and space blanket combination, is a lean-to with its back to the wind and a reflector fire directing heat into the shelter (an example of this can be seen in Figure

8–1 in chapter 8). Use a sheet of aluminum foil, a wall of green tree limbs, rocks, and so forth as a reflector. The all-night fire can keep a lean-to reasonably warm as long as there is enough wood. As the fire begins to die, simply toss on enough wood to keep it going another few hours.

When rain, snow, volcanic ash, or a solar storm are not a threat, a reflector fire directing heat toward a large rock or dirt bank that is also blocking the wind can make for a nice place to sleep. The heat is reflected toward the rock or bank and back onto you while you sleep. You have heat from two sides.

You can build a fire on the spot you plan to sleep on and let it warm the earth for a few hours, then rake the fire away to a new spot and sleep on the warm earth. If you have a means of digging, you can dig a shallow hole where you plan to lie, shovel in a bed of hot ashes and cover all the ashes with a layer of 3 to 5 inches (7 to 23 centimeters) of soil. Make sure to cover all of the ashes and check to ensure you have enough soil over them before lying down. You don't want to have a too hot or too cold bed. Using coals and ashes are an energy consuming means of having a warm bed.

If you find yourself without a space blanket, sleeping bag, or blankets, you can use dry dead grass, leaves, or evergreen boughs to provide some protection from the cold. Remember that insulation is dead air space and anything that will create dead air space will help keep you warm. The rain suit can offer a lot of warmth when sleeping due to its ability to stop the wind from hitting your skin. Also, stuffing dead, dry grass or leaves inside your rain suit between your rain suit and your clothes, can make it into a makeshift sleeping bag. Be resourceful.

Fire

In a national disaster survival situation, the ability to start a fire can make the difference between living and dying. That is why a fire is third on your survival priority list. During your walkout, there will be times when you and/or your family will be scared, embarrassed, lonely, hungry, cold, being attacked by flying pests, confused, and usually in poor spirits. A fire will keep you and the family busy. It will also help drive away pests, provide warmth, purify water, dry clothes, lift spirits, cook food, give light, and may be used in crafting many useful items. Fire gives a sense of security and, in a way, provides company. Flame can harden a wooden spear point. The ash from the fireplace can be used for the following:

- Small amounts of the white ashes can be consumed to overcome constipation.
- Small amounts of the black ashes can be consumed to stop diarrhea.
- Lye (used to make soap) is made from wood ash.

In short, fire is one of the most valuable aids in your safe walkout.

At the same time, fire can cause problems. Unwanted observers or passersby can detect the smoke and the light it produces. It can cause forest fires or destroy essential equipment. Fire can also cause burns and carbon monoxide poisoning when used in shelters. That is why it is so important for you to understand the need for fire and always remember to weigh your need for fire against your need to avoid detection.

Another thing to is to have two fires in your camp. Build one fire to provide warmth near your sleeping area. Build a second one nearby for cooking: scraps of food dropped on the ground during cooking and afterwards can attract unwanted hungry animals into your camp area.

Except the Unexpected

Always expect the unexpected—no matter what. Or you might find yourself in the next situation. It's late afternoon and you have decided to stop. You take off your backpack, dig out your waterproof match container and fire starter, and build a fire. Sounds easy, doesn't it? But what if you didn't have matches? What if you didn't know how to build a fire? Then there is the inexperienced person who saw people starting fires on TV and might say you can always start a fire with flint and steel, with sticks using the bow-drill method, or with lens from your glasses. That inexperienced person might also say anybody can build a fire. How wrong and dangerous this kind of thinking can be.

Except for a handful of experts, there are few people among us who can start a fire without matches or a lighter. Even the magnesium lighter recommended for your backpack takes practice to master. And flint and steel, the bow-drill method, and some of the other fire starting techniques discussed later in this chapter make interesting demonstrations but seldom work in a real survival camp. They also use a lot of energy. Despite what many survival books say, there are few substitutes for fresh, dry, wooden strike-anywhere kitchen matches, cigarette lighters, and prepackaged fire starters. In your case, practice using the magnesium fire starter, for matches will become another one of those items remembered during the "good times."

It might sound silly, but make sure you practice using them, and not just on nice days. Far too many people think that with matches, cigarette lighters, or a magnesium fire starters, they can build a fire. That is not true. When you've added the stress of your walkout and the physical exertion of a long day of walking, you could become exhausted by the mere effort of starting a fire. And seldom will our walkout happen during ideal weather. The walkout situation will be accompanied by bad weather, volcanic ash, high windstorms, solar storms—the worst calamity of weather you could imagine. You will have to know how to build a fire in wet, windy, and cold conditions that make fire building difficult at best. Only people with experience in fire building will pull it off. Do I have to say again how much practice is needed?

Preparation

Look for a dry spot that is protected from the wind and suitably placed in relation to your shelter. If possible, ensure the location will concentrate the heat in the direction you desire. Have a supply of wood or other fuel available.

If you are in a wooded or brush-covered area, clear the brush and scrape the surface soil from the spot you have selected. Clear a circle at least 3 feet (1 meter) in diameter so there is little chance of the fire spreading.

To aid in the heating process, construct a fire wall using logs or rocks. This wall will help reflect and direct the heat where you want it. (See Figure 8-1.) It will also reduce flying sparks and cut down on the amount of wind blowing into the fire. However, you will need enough wind to keep the fire burning.

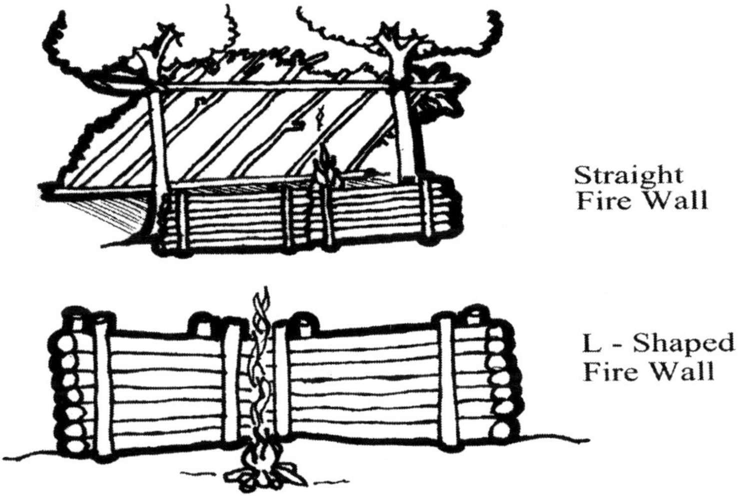

Figure 8 - 1 Types of Fire Walls

In some situations, you may find that an underground fireplace will best meet your needs. It conceals the fire and serves well for cooking food. To make an underground fireplace or Dakota fire hole (see Figure 8-2):

1. Dig a hole in the ground.
2. On the upwind side of this hole, poke or dig a large connecting hole for ventilation.
3. Build your fire in the hole as illustrated.

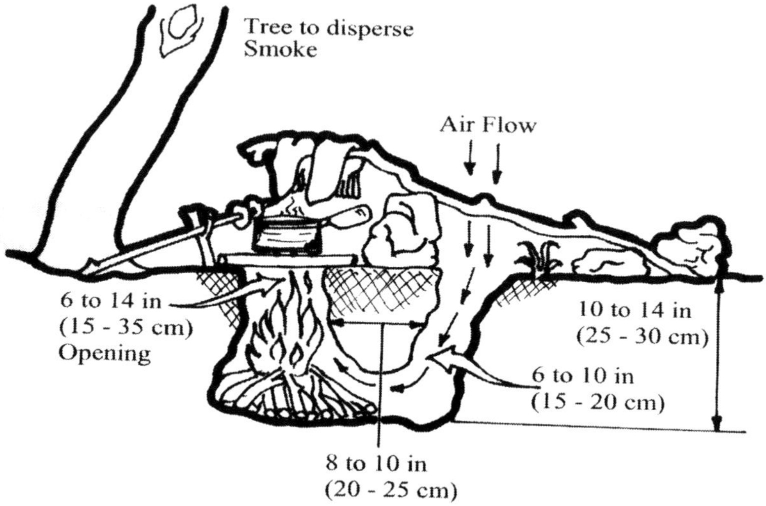

Figure 8 - 2 Dakota Fire Hole

If you are in a snow-covered area, use green logs to make a dry base for your fire. (See Figure 8-3.) Trees with wrist-sized trunks are easily broken in extreme cold. Cut or break several green logs and lay them side-by-side on top of the snow. Add one or two more layers. Lay the top layer of logs opposite those below it.

Figure 8 - 3 Base for Fire in Snow-covered Area

How to Build A Fire

Of the many variations of fire construction, these are the ones I use the most:

Teepee fire—The tinder and kindling is arranged in a conical shape, like a teepee, for quick ignition. (See Figure 8-4.) This type of fire burns quickly and uses fuel fast!

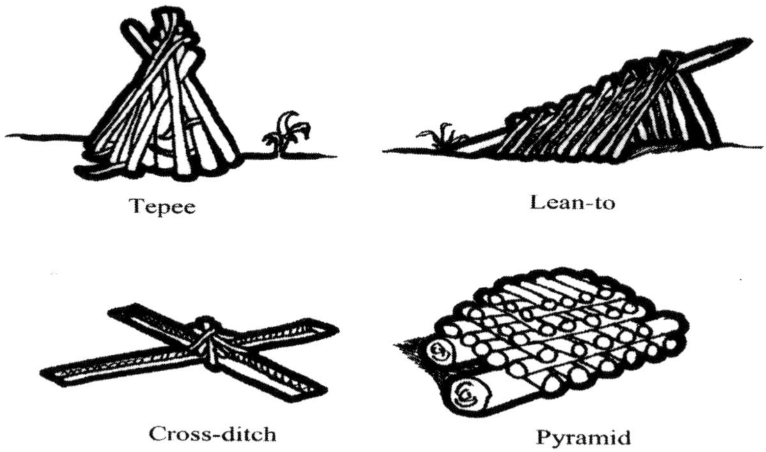

Figure 8 - 4 Methods for Constructing Fires

Lean-to—To make this fire (see Figure 8-4), push a green stick into the ground at a 30-degree angle with the end of the stick pointed in the direction of the wind. Lean pieces of kindling against the lean-to stick and then place some tinder inside, under this lean-to stick. Light the tinder. As the kindling catches fire from the tinder, add more kindling.

Cross-ditch—To use this method (see Figure 8-4), scratch a cross about 1 foot (30 centimeters) in size in the ground. Dig the cross 3 inches (7.5 centimeters) deep. Put a large wad of tinder in the middle of the cross. Build a kindling pyramid above the tinder. The shallow ditch allows air to sweep under the tinder to provide a draft. This type of fire is a fast burning, hot fire.

Pyramid or log cabin fire—The kindling is stacked one layer over another, largest pieces on bottom and smallest on top, with the tinder placed underneath. This fire (see Figure 8-4) will burn downward, requiring less attention at night.

Crisscross fire—By placing the layers of wood in a crisscross pattern, this type of fire can be used to dry wet wood placed on the top row. Drying wood protects the burning wood and makes it a slower burning fire. It looks like the example in figure 8-3, the base for fire in a snow-covered area.

No matter which style you use, experiment and find the one that works best for you and your situation.

Steps to building a fire—Understand that you don't start a fire—you build it. There are five things you need to build a fire successfully:

1. Fire must have oxygen, since burning is nothing more than rapid oxidation.
2. Fire must have source of heat: a match, cigarette lighter, or magnesium lighter provides this.
3. Fire must have tinder to catch the flame of the match or fire starter to start the fire. One source is your pre-packed fire starter, whether purchased from a store, homemade, or a cotton ball fire starter spoken of later in this chapter. Another excellent fire starter, if you are around pine trees, is pine sap. Add to that natural tinder such as a bird's nest, bark, cedar bark, down from thistle, pinecones, or dried grass. Even fine steel wool has been used as tinder when the strands are pulled apart loosely. The use of pine sap or pine pitch will also burn hot enough to dry out and ignite small pieces of wet wood.
4. You will need small sticks and twigs to catch the fire from the tinder, thus making it hotter.
5. You will need dry, dead fuel wood—more of it than you would think. Dry, dead wood can be hard to find in wet weather, but some can usually be found on the lower limbs of evergreen trees, in standing dead timber, or by splitting wet logs or large limbs and getting to their dry wood interiors. And do not forget animal dung as a source of fuel for the fire. On the other hand, the white driftwood found along rivers and lakeshores looks good and catches easy (makes great tinder), but there is no heat value to that kind of wood.

Are you ready? If you think you are, then answer this question: Can you build a fire with one match when you are cold, shaking, wet, tired, and scared? If your answer is anything but a definite "yes," then you need to practice! This is the time to master the art, not when it really counts during your walkout.

How to Light a Fire

Always light your fire from the upwind side. Make sure to lay your tinder, kindling, and fuel so that your fire will burn as long as you need it. Igniters provide the initial heat required to start the tinder burning. Several methods are:

Matches—Make sure these matches are waterproof. Also, store them in a waterproof container along with a dependable striker pad.

Cotton ball fire starter—This easy-to-use fire starter is made from cotton balls and petroleum jelly. Moderately cover a cotton ball with petroleum jelly, place in a plastic bag, and set it in the sun so the cotton ball can absorb the jelly. Another way is to place the jelly-coated cotton balls on a cookie sheet and place them in an oven heated to 100 to 120 degrees. After the cotton balls sponge up the petroleum jelly, place them in sealable plastic bag and throw the bag in you backpack.

When you are ready to use one of the cotton balls to light a fire, take a single cotton ball and pull it part, and stretch it to make it thin. Light it with a match, cigarette, convex lens, or the striker side of the magnesium lighter. If the cotton ball has absorbed the petroleum jelly correctly, the slightest spark will ignite it, the cotton ball will burn for several minutes.

Magnesium fire starter—Place a flat, dry leaf under your tinder, leaving a portion of the leaf exposed. Using the blade side of your knife make several scrapes along the magnesium side of the lighter depositing the scrapings on the exposed leaf. Then turn the magnesium lighter over and with the backside of your knife, scrape downward along the bar and create sparks that fall on the magnesium shavings on the leaf. The sparks will ignite the magnesium, which ignites the tinder.

Gunpowder—Often you will have ammunition with you. If so, carefully extract the bullet from the shell casing, and with a leaf under your tinder, pour the gunpowder on the exposed leaf and up on the tinder. A spark will ignite the powder. Be extremely careful when extracting the bullet from the case.

Flint and steel—Similar to the magnesium starter, this uses the direct spark method. You strike a flint or other hard, sharp-edged rock with a piece of carbon steel (stainless steel will not produce a good spark). This method requires practice to learn the art of producing a spark and getting that spark to land where you want it to land. When a spark has caught in the tinder, gently blow on it. The spark will glow brighter, spread, and burst into flames.

Convex lens—Use this method (see Figure 8-5) only on bright, sunny days. Use a lens from binoculars, a camera, telescopic sights, or a magnifying glasses. Angle the lens to concentrate the sun's rays on the tinder, holding it there until the tinder begins to smolder. Gently blow or fan the tinder into flame. If you have already constructed one of the previous shown fires, carefully move and apply the tinder to the additional tender at the base of your constructed fire. If you have not constructed a fire, then start adding smaller pieces of wood; continue adding as you gradually increase the size of the pieces of wood.

Figure 8 - 5 Lens Method of Fire Starting

Fire plow—This is a friction method of ignition. (See Figure 8-6.) You rub a hardwood shaft against a softer wood base. To use this method, cut a straight groove in the base. Before you start plowing the blunt tip of the shaft up and down the groove, fine tinder on the ground in front of the base of the groove. The friction from the plowing action ignites the wood particles as they fall on the tinder.

Figure 8 - 6 Fire-plow

Bow and drill—The technique of starting a fire with a bow and drill (see Figure 8-7) is simple, but you must exert much effort and be persistent (or should I say: Patience, patience, and more patience) to produce a fire. You need the following items to build a fire using this method:

- *Bow*—When building a fire using this method, the bow needs to be a resilient, green stick about 1 inch (2.5 centimeters) in diameter and about 1.5 to 2 feet (45 to 60 centimeters) long. The type of wood is not important as long as it is green. The bowstring can be any type of cordage (your parachute cord or the string that makes up the cord, or even your shoe laces). You tie the bowstring from one end of the bow to the other, without any slack.
- *Socket*—The socket is an easily grasped stone, piece of hardwood, or a bone with a slight depression in one side. Use it to hold the drill in place and to apply downward pressure.
- *Drill*—The drill should be a straight, seasoned, hardwood stick about 1 inch (2 centimeters) in diameter and 10 to 12 inches (25 centimeters) long. The top end is pointed to reduce friction with the socket and the low end blunt to produce more friction. To help the process go as smooth as possible, use a straight drill. If the drill is not straight, whittle it as straight as possible.
- *Fire board*—Its size is up to you. A seasoned softwood board of any available wood around you that is about 1 inch (2.5 centimeters) thick and 4 inches (10 centimeters) wide is preferable. Cut a depression about 1 inch (2 centimeters) from the edge on one side of the board. On the underside, make a V-shaped cut from the edge of the board almost the center of the depression. (Refer to the blown-up view in Figure 8-7.)

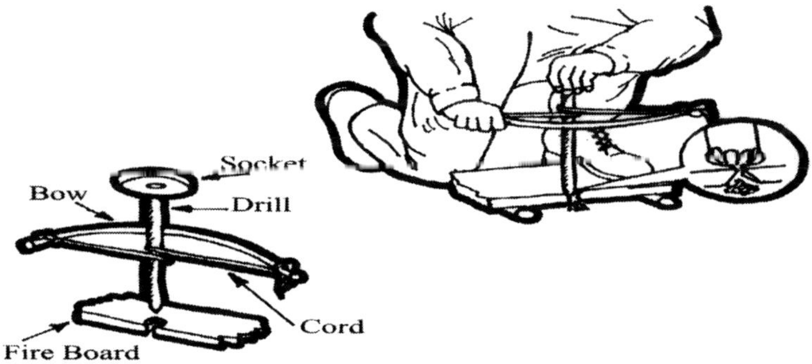

Figure 8 - 7 Bow and Drill

Before you use the bow and drill, construct your fire, ensuring you leave adequate space to place the bundle of tinder you will ignite with this method. Start by raising the fire board off the ground by placing it on a couple of branches. Once that is completed, put a small bundle of tinder on a piece of wood or large leaf under the V-shaped cut in the fire board. Place one foot on the fire board to keep it from moving. Loop the bowstring over the drill and place the drill in the precut depression on the fire board. Place the socket, held in one hand, on the top of the drill to hold it in position. Press down on the drill and saw the bow back and forth to twirl the drill. (See Figure 8-7.) Once you have established a smooth motion, apply more downward pressure and work the bow faster. This action will grind hot black powder into the tinder, causing a spark to catch. Then softly blow on the tinder until it ignites. Carefully move the tinder to your constructed fire and continue to feed your fire.

> **Note**—The bow and drill, and the fire plow methods are exhaustive and require practice to ensure success.

If you can, find someone that has done this and have him or her teach you. It'll save you hours of grief! Practice makes perfect. Do this at home in your spare time, and learn how to do it! Do it several times and you will always know how to do it. And if you have a good spark, the tinder will literally burst into flames so be ready with the rest of your fire before actually lighting it. Above all else, practice while you have the time to spar: this is not a process to learn during your walkout to your safe haven.

Fire coal carrier—This may be another method to keep in mind if you find yourself without any kind of fire starter, like if your backpack was lost, stolen, or left behind.

Once you start a fire by one of the means we have previously discussed, find an animal horn or bone that can be partially filled with fine tinder (animal hair, feathers, a mix of green and dry grass) and a coal from the fire so you can carry it with you until you stop to camp for the evening.

What you want to happen is for the coal to receive just enough oxygen to smolder in the tinder all day. Have patience; it may take several tries before you master this method.

I want to reiterate a safety precaution: Since you and yours will be part of the millions traveling to various safe havens, or wandering in-search of a safe haven, be wary. Think. Be watchful. Teach this to your family. *Always* cover your tracks by trying to leave the camp area as it looked when you arrived. Be ever vigilant, for there will be bad people doing bad things to whomever they find.

Food

Normally I would have started talking about food that is already available in the home; but every time the subject of survival was brought up, the discussion usually revolved around finding edible food in the wild and how to procure it. We are obsessed with eating. It has been proven many times that most of us can go without eating several weeks, if necessary, and not die. Most of us carry around an abundance of fat that could keep us alive for a long period of time.

For those of you who think you cannot survive without eating three meals a day, I would suggest you read and study the many survival and other books that describe and show detailed photos of the approximately 2,000 edible wild plants and 700 toxic wild plants found in North America. Distinguishing one from the other requires a lot of field experience during all four seasons.

Wild Plant Edibility Test

If for some reason you find yourself in a situation where you think you must eat wild plants but don't know which ones are edible, the Edibility Test discussed in all the United States Military survival guides may be of some help:

1. Never eat mushrooms or fungi.
2. Poisonous plant life means all parts, including flowers, can be toxic. Use caution with plants having these characteristics:
   » milky or discolored sap
   » spines or fine hairs
   » bitter or soapy taste

- » beans or bulbs
- » white or red berries
- » shiny leaves
- » umbrella flowers

3. Take a small mouthful, chew it, and retain it in the mouth. Wait five minutes for any effects such as burning, stinging, or numbing.
4. If there are none, swallow and wait eight hours for any effects such as diarrhea, cramps, pains, numbing, vomiting, and so forth to manifest themselves.
5. If there are none, repeat the process using a handful of the plant, and wait another eight hours for ill effects.
6. If no ill effects occur, the plant is considered safe to eat.

Keep in mind that any new or strange food should be eaten with restraint until your body's digestive system has become accustom to it. Also, don't expect wild plants to taste good—many don't and others are almost tasteless. And it takes some adjustment to get your stomach to accept a diet of wild plants.

Some other things you need to know about wild plants:

1. Plants you see animals eating may be toxic to humans. For example, deer love to eat poison ivy, and birds eat berries that are poisonous to humans. Therefore, do not assume you can eat unknown plants or berries just because you see the animals eating them.
2. Plants that may be edible in one stage of its growth cycle may not be edible in another, such as pokeweed. Or a plant may taste sweet in the spring and bitter in late summer, like the dandelion plant.
3. Plants that contain one edible part may be toxic on other parts, such as the wild plum. Another is the common tomato plant.

Edible Wild Animals

If you find yourself in a position where you must resort to wild foods to avoid starving to death, then wild animals may be a better choice. With practice and with even more patience, the hunting and trapping of animals will become a natural skill. North America has a good population of wild animals, both large and small, that are edible. The initial trick is to catch them before you can cook them.

Depending upon the time of year and where you are geographically, there is some form of animal that you can eat after you catch and kill it. At the same time, insects, small aquatic animals, and fish may be the easiest to gather and highest in protein. Your main goal here is to have patience, patience, and then more patience, as you learn the day-to-day habits of the animal world that you have always lived within.

Use the time you have now to experiment and learn how to trap both land and aquatic animals.

Food Prior to the Walkout

In an earlier chapter we discussed the difference between a *consumer survivalist* and a *survivor.* We talked about how the consumer survivalist attacks the process and in that process sets himself up. Instead of going hog-wild, use the time left to slowly prepare. Focus on buying a supply of canned goods and dry goods that can be stored in the house: in a pantry or in a back closet. Date the items and as you slowly increase your supply, and remember to rotate the newer stock to the back and use the older stock in your everyday consumption of food. This approach will not place the family in danger of telling a secret, for it will become a normal day-to-day process of having extra food set aside. And telling the truth can be a good thing: "The price of food has gone up so much, I've decided to save money by buying larger quantities during weekly sales."

You may also want to learn how to pickle food.

What is pickling? Pickling is the process of preserving food by soaking the food in a brine solution usually consisting of a mixture of sugar and salt in water to produce lactic acid, or marinating and storing the food in an acid solution, usually vinegar (acetic acid). The acid and salt change the composition of the meat, fish or vegetables into a food which is both desirable and gives it a longer shelf life.

Note—This could turn into another home business adventure.

An American pickling recipe—This recipe is for marinated mushroom, but you can substitute meat, fish or other vegetables in place of the mushrooms.

American Pickling Recipe

6 cups water
1 tsp. sugar
2 Tbsp. coarse (kosher) salt

½ small cinnamon stick
1½ pound small white mushrooms, rinsed
½ tsp. whole black peppercorns
¾ cup mild white wine vinegar
½ tsp. dried thyme
1 Tbsp. coriander seeds
1 clove garlic, peeled and halved
2 bay leaves
¾ cup olive oil (approx.)

Combine water and 1 tablespoon of the salt in a saucepan and bring to a boil. Add the mushrooms and boil for 2 minutes, then drain, reserving ⅔ cup of liquid. In an enameled, Pyrex, or stainless steel saucepan, combine reserved mushroom liquid, vinegar, coriander seeds, bay leaves, cinnamon, peppercorns, thyme, and the remaining 1 tablespoon of salt. Boil for 5 minutes. Pack the cooked mushrooms into a clean quart jar and pour the pickling liquid over them. Add the garlic clove and then add the olive oil, using whatever amount is necessary to fill the jar, and then cap the jar. You can store in a cool, dark place (pantry or basement), or refrigerate for at least a week before serving. Shake the jar at least once a day. Once opened, the marinated mushrooms will keep for several weeks (refrigerated).

A pickling recipe from India—Indian pickles are a variety of spicy preserved vegetables or fruit. To make this recipe, clean and finely chop seasonal vegetables and fruits. Mix with a personal blend of ground spices and marinate in sesame (gingelly) oil, mustard oil, or lemon juice, instead of using vinegar.

Pickles are generally stored in porcelain or glass jars with airtight lids. The acidic nature of the marinade retards bacterial growth, while the oil acts as a preservative. Pickles can retain their freshness and flavor as long as they do not come into contact with moisture.

Another thing to think about is acquiring items like spices, salt, pepper, tooth paste, baking soda, along with over-the-counter allergy, diarrhea, and first-aid medications—all of this will be invaluable for barter.

Food for the Walkout

Waking up in the morning and making oatmeal is a cheery way to start a camping day, because you have plenty of time to start a fire and prepare the oatmeal, and clean the pot and utensils.

When packing food for a walkout, keep in mind that you will be walking out—not camping out. Instead of spending lazy days camped next to a babbling brook, you will be grieving, you will be dealing with other people in shock or even emotionally shutdown, and your mind will be filled with finding safety for yourself and your loved ones.

In a world rocked by disaster, water will be scarce and the smoke from a fire will give away your location. Therefore, you need finger foods with a fairly balanced ratio of protein, fats, and carbohydrates that you can eat on the move, because you're walking to save your life and the lives of your loved ones, you are dealing with a roller coaster of upheavals each day until you reach your safe haven. With this in mind, here are some simple things you need in your pack, in addition to a variety of pickled food.

Beef jerky—A great on-the-go food that stores well. While you can buy it in bulk, a better idea is to make your own. There are great jerky recipe books, so buy one and experiment—that way you'll have a mix of interesting flavors.

When it comes to homemade jerky, many people are concerned with its longevity before it spoils. If prepared correctly, the beef jerky will turn to dust before it spoils. To ensure you prepare it correctly, a butcher friend of mine explained that you have to cut the raw beef in very thin strips. He explained the reason for the thin strips, less than a ¼ of an inch, was to prevent the flies from lying eggs in the unprepared meat. The next thing is to dry the meat with a low heat, not cook with a high heat.

The easiest way to make beef jerky, while at home, is to set your oven at 100 to 120 degrees and leave the thin strips of beef in for about 24 hours. The meat is not supposed to cook, it's supposed to dry. While on the walkout, set up a rack made from limbs or other construction material alongside the fire. Hang the thin strips of meat on the rack and allow it to dry (different flavored tastes can be created by the use of different types of wood). A good piece of jerky is bone-dry, and hard enough to kill you if you filed the end to a point. It will also keep practically for ever.

Beef jerky alone is too limited a diet to keep a human being alive forever. That is why the fat from the beef is pounded into pemmican.

Pemmican—Pemmican is a Native American word roughly translated as "travel food for long trips." It is a compact source of concentrated energy that needs no preparation on the trail. It is basically made from dried beef (or any kind of meat), rendered fat, berries, and anything else that is nutritious and available (including dried insects, discussed later in this chapter). It gives the body the densest nutritional value in a simple, hand-feeding manner. And it's high in energy ingredients that keep one from being hungry, and feeds the body everything it needs. For more information, look it up on the Internet.

Meat Pemmican—To make meat pemmican, you will need 2 to 6 pounds of meat. You will also need suet (animal fat or bacon fat) of human-consumption grade. Make sure to ask for this, or they will give you bird-feed grade. Last, you will need about one cup dried cherries (you can also use cranberries, blueberries, or any kind of dried fruit or vegetables).

To make pemmican:

1. After the meat dries into jerky, remove it from the oven (or from the rack) and place several pieces in a blender (or another source while on your walkout). Add a small handful of dried cherries or other dried fruits or vegetables. The whole thing will pulverize into a stringy, blended jerky powder.
2. Cook the fat over *very* low heat. If you have a gas stove, consider using a flame diffuser to further reduce the flame. Make sure the fat is melted but do not burn the liquid fat.
3. Combine the blended jerky powder and fat, in a ratio of about two parts jerky powder to one part fat. Pour the liquid fat over the blended jerky mixture. This will soak into the meat, but you want a very slightly moist material, not wet, runny, or too dry. Stir the drier meat into the wetter meat so everything is fully coated and the fat has soaked into everything.
4. Make small patties and pack in airtight containers; Cleaned intestine, sausage casings, or glass or plastic containers can be used.
5. Store in a cool, dry, dark place.

Word of caution—Pemmican is a concentrated food that is best consumed sparingly, when you are active, and not for an extended period of time. Consumption of hard fat can be unhealthy for inactive people, and protein over-consumption can overload the body with uric acid (which may lead to gout) and calcium oxalate (the mineral which forms kidney stones). Ketones may also build up in the system, causing kidney damage. (A sign of protein over-consumption is ketone breath, which smells like nail polish or overripe pineapple.)

Meatless Pemmican—To make this you will need:

½ cup raisins

½ cup dried pumpkin or squash

½ cup peanuts
½ cup acorn or corn meal
½ cup hickory nuts
⅓ cup honey or maple syrup
½ cup dried apples

In order to make sure that the acorn or corn meal is bone-dry, spread it in a thin layer on a cookie sheet and place it in a warm oven for 15–30 minutes, checking frequently. The oven should be at the lowest possible setting. Then combine the dry ingredients and either chop them with a knife or grind them coarsely through a food grinder. Add the honey or maple syrup and blend thoroughly. Divide the mixture into ¼ cup portions, press into cakes, and seal in airtight containers. Store in a cool, dry, dark place, or store in the refrigerator for easy access.

Word of caution—Such fiber will have a "bathroom" effect, and it will be very high in energy from the sugars in the honey and fruit. However, the excellent fats and proteins from the nuts will help counter the overabundance of energy.

Stuffed bread—This is very similar to pemmican but does not need to be cooked. It is made of dried fruit and berries (your choice) stuffed into hard roll bread about the size of a hotdog bun of either oat or rye. Nip one end off, use a knife or the handle of a spoon and puncture an opening from one end to the other in the middle of the bun. Stuff it with your choice of dried fruits and/or berries. Now it is ready to be soaked in honey, and then placed on a rack to allow the outside to dry. Place in an airtight container to preserve it. Just like pemmican, it is high in energy; a person could walk all day on just a few mouthfuls, providing there's water to help wash each bite down.

Hardtack—This simple type of cracker or biscuit is made from flour, water, and salt. Inexpensive and long lasting, it is and was used for sustenance in the absence of perishable foods, commonly during long sea voyages and military campaigns.

Historically, in 1801, a Boston merchant started making hardtack made of flour and water that would not deteriorate during long sea voyages, which was also used extensively by gold miners immigrating to the gold fields of California and Alaska. Later, both sides of the Civil War used hardtack as a main source of food. Not only was it known as hardtack, it was also called pilot bread, ship's biscuit, sea biscuit, sea bread, or (pejoratively) dog biscuit. The name derives from the British sailor slang for food, "tack," and the crackers or biscuits have been called "tooth dullers," "sheet iron," or "molar breakers."

Because it is so hard and dry, it will keep for years as long as it is kept dry, and transported hardtack will survive rough handling and endure extremes of temperature. To soften hardtack, dunk in water, brine, coffee, broth or soup, some other liquid, or cook into a skillet meal.

United States Army Cavalry Hardtack

4 cups flour
2 tsp. sea salt
1 cup water (add more if needed)

Mix ingredients, adding water until it becomes a pasty dough. Flour and salt a cookie sheet. Spread hardtack mix to an even layer, about ¼ of an inch or less. Cut into 2-inch squares, or smaller. Lightly salt tops and dust with flour. Bake at 350 degrees for about 1 hour, until light brown. Turn oven down to 200 degrees and bake for at least 4 hours or until no moisture remains. Once cooled, pack away in an airtight container to keep it dry and dust free.

Note—Up until the early to mid 1900s, flour was full of natural minerals and vitamins, and when baked into bread it contained everything you and I basically needed to live. Then manufactures started bleaching flour, achieving the white look we have today. In that bleaching process, all natural minerals and vitamins are removed, leaving the flour with no real food value (the same thing is done to salt, which is why I use sea salt). Because of the bleaching process, I would recommend you use non-processed flour found at whole food stores, natural food stores, or from a local mill. You can also substitute flour with a non-processed rye or rice flour and you can even add finely ground dried beef jerky and other finely ground dried vegetables, fruits, or insects to the recipe (discussed in the next section referred to as "trail tack"). Just remember the proper mixture renders the hardtack a solid puck, solid, hard and indestructive until you need it.

Trail tack—This is my name for the modifications I made to the hardtack recipe. The first thing I did was exchange wheat flour for cornmeal. This modification worked well, producing a product that tasted like hard, salty cornbread. Due to the coarseness of the cornmeal, the trail tack broke apart easier than the original hardtack.

The second change, and the one I like best, was taking some of the homemade beef jerky, along with dried tomatoes and carrots, and grinding them into a coarse powder and adding them to the hardtack recipe.

When it came to cooking them, I deposit tablespoon-size balls of the mixture on the cookie sheet and then flatten them to look like cookies, ending up with a silver dollar size hard cracker. This version is a little easier to eat and tastes a lot better.

Another thing I did was mix rice flour and half-and-half with the wheat flour. This modification added more minerals and nutrients to the recipe. If you want, you could use rice flour instead of wheat flour. To me, rice flour tastes better.

Dried fruits and vegetables—Another great on-the-go food. While you can buy them in bulk, a better idea is to buy a home food dehydrator and make your own. Experiment with various types of fruit; apples, bananas, oranges, lemons, grapes, strawberries, coconut meat, and so forth. Even try vegetables such as tomatoes, carrots, squash, onions, or garlic—try them all!

Dried or smoked fish—High in protein and good omega fats, this type of fish can be purchased already dried and/or smoked. Or you can modify the beef jerky recipes to include fish, keeping in mind that some people prefer to soak the fish in vinegar or straight lemon juice to add additional flavor before drying or smoking.

Canned sardines and spam—Though a little heavier, this is food you can serve on the first few days of your walkout, reducing the weight of your backpacks, and easing the stress a bit by giving yourself the feeling of being on a picnic.

Peanut butter and crackers—Nuts are a popular snack food, but need special handling and storage to keep them from going rancid. Also, most contain pungent or bitter aromatic oils and ferments, which make them hard to digest. That is the last thing you need on a long walk.

Instead of nuts and trail mix, pack a small, unopened jar of any brand of creamy style peanut butter and some crackers. It is a rich source of easy-to-digest protein, especially for diabetics and those with dental issues. Avoid natural style peanut butter because it separates in the jar.

Dark chocolate—Dark chocolate bars with cocoa solids content of 70 percent or more are good to have. The best are with pure cocoa butter, and are very nutritious. The caffeine in the chocolate is a helpful pick-me-up and will help keep your spirits up. Dark chocolate is also similar to codeine used for suppressing persistent coughs, and helps reduce hunger.

Hoodia tablets—A popular weight loss supplement, indigenous people originally used Hoodia for energy and to curb appetite on long treks where meals were few and far between. Due to the selling of counterfeit Hoodia products over the Internet, your best bet is to buy locally from a reputable merchant.

Even though most of the food items discussed should have long shelf lives, they should be inspected periodically to make sure none of them have gone rancid. And remember: Every ounce of weight counts. So, pack, try it out, re-pack, and try it again. Now it's time to hit the trail and enjoy the time we have by going camping for the weekend.

Nature's Supermarket

No matter how well we prepare, things will happen: you may experience unexpected delays, or your walkout route will become inaccessible. Whatever the reason, you find yourself running short on supplies. What do you do?

Over the years, I have read numerous news reports concerning people who actually starved to death in the wild because they did not know how to go shopping for natural food. When we enter "nature's supermarket," most of us may be lost in more ways than one. The foods we are used to seeing just aren't there; or at least they don't look the same way we would expect them to look. Keep in mind that many of the foods we now purchase were once, and may still be, wild in the woods. What do you know about vegetables? Do you know that certain vegetables grow underground and some on top of the ground? Nonetheless, many folks have no idea what is edible and what isn't once they leave the house.

I suggest you do some research and find out as much about wilderness food procurement as you can. And, since it is very likely the most common things in the bush will supply a large portion of our "survival stew," lets look at natural food sources a little closer.

Edible insects—If it is not winter, you may be able to rustle up a nice meal of insects. They are usually out in abundance and all you have to do is gather them up. What? You don't like the idea of eating bugs? Common sense tells us that insects are usually there and we are hungry, so why not get together for a meal? Now I have to admit, bugs aren't my favorite meal, but they can help keep you alive.

Insects are very rich in fat and protein, both of which are important to the walkout survival process. While many insects may be eaten raw, most people prefer them cooked (in some cases, like ants, cooking should be done to remove poisons). I personally think the best way to cook them is to add them to a "survival stew," which is a mix of all the various things you were able to find that day. On the larger insects, remove the wings and legs. I suggest you do this so the sharp spines on the legs don't injure your throat or cause you to choke while swallowing. I do not recommend the beginner bite into an insect. It is like biting a piece of candy filled with a special middle, but without the great taste. It is important to consider the fact that most of our aversion to the eating of insects is cultural and psychological. In many cultures, insects are eaten regularly.

Insects can be found under rocks, inside of dead logs, obviously on anthills, and in nooks and crannies. Be extra careful when looking for insects, because snakes, scorpions and other biting or stinging critters like to stay in the same places. Wear gloves if you have them and use caution while shopping for dinner. Avoid placing your hands in dark holes or other places you cannot see. Make noise, and keep your eyes scanning from side to side to avoid snakes.

Avoid any insects that are found in animal carcasses, dung, or trash. They may carry diseases or parasites. Also, try to avoid any insect you see that has a bright body color or is hairy. Some may be eaten, but many are poisonous. It is easier to remember to just avoid them, than try to identify those that are safe to eat. You should be able to find plenty of worms, ants, grasshoppers, and other bugs to make a meal.

Worms—These may be eaten raw or cooked. I suggest you rinse them off to avoid getting the sand or dirt grit in your teeth. Do not confuse worms with grubs—there is a difference. Some grubs, especially those found on the underside of leaves, may contain toxins. I would suggest you avoid them; but, worms can be dried, crushed, and then added to soups or just eaten raw.

Grubs—Most of the various types of grubs are edible and very good for you. But as I mentioned in the previous paragraph, some of the leaf-crawling type may contain toxins that could make you sick or even cause death. Do your own research and find out which are which.

Mealworms—Mealworms are one of the easiest to eat. You don't really have to clean mealworms, though if you want, you can chop off their heads before eating them raw. As mentioned before, if you struggle with the idea of eating them raw, place them by the fire and cook them first before eating, or adding them to the meal.

Mosquito eggs or larva—If you live in a geographical area where mosquitoes are plentiful, take advantage (or if you prefer to take revenge) of the bounty of eggs found floating in shallow waters and gather them up. Most people dry the eggs and use them as additives to supplement daily meals. And while you are at it, keep an eye out for frog eggs too.

Ants—Ants, on the other hand, may have a painful bite (formic acid). However, by cooking them for about six or seven minutes, the toxins are destroyed. Then they may be eaten as is or added to soups. There is only one real problem with this readily-available food source: it takes a whole lot of ants to make a meal. And while you are at it, do not forget the ant larva, those white egg-sacks found around ant hills are young unborn ants. No matter which ones you gather, they add protein and fat to your diet. Keep in mind; even the huge grizzly bear eats them.

Grasshoppers—Grasshoppers can be knocked from the air with a shirt, fishing net, or with a piece of cloth. Remember to remove the wings, antennae, and legs before eating them. I suggest they be placed on a flat rock near the fire and cooked. Or if you have a pot, pan, skillet, or an empty can, roast them in the container. Once cooked, they may be added to soups or stews. Some people prefer to crush them and dry them into a powder before eating them. The method you use is up to you. Of course, some people are capable of sitting around a campfire late at night eating them raw as you might eat potato chips. I have not been able to completely overcome my squeamishness of eating raw grasshoppers, but if I had to eat them to survive, bring on the meal!

Crickets—These are as plentiful as grasshoppers. Cricket's heads, hind legs, and wing cases can be removed according to personal preference, since cricket legs tend to get stuck in your teeth. And based on personal preference, crickets can be eaten raw or cooked.

Snakes—If you happen to see a snake, very carefully kill it with a large rock or long stick. Then carefully cut the head off (the head and fangs are still dangerous even when removed from the body), gut it lengthwise, skin it, and cut it into cubes. At that point I suggest it be added to the stew pot for the day. I usually bury a poisonous snakes head in a hole at lest 12" deep. That keeps others from stepping on the head, which still contains the fangs and poison. If you are unsure if the snake is poisonous or not, then treat it at all times as if it is poisonous. And, yes, both poisonous and non-poisonous snakes can be eaten safely.

Eggs—The best thing to remember, whether they be bird, frog, fish, snake, alligator, eggs is that eggs are eggs.

Fowl—Any domestic or wild fowl can be on the menu. From sparrows, to robins, to ducks, pheasants, turkeys, and hens, all of them will taste great in the evening stew.

Squirrel—Like rabbit, the squirrel and its close cousin the rat, tastes like chicken when cooked over an open fire.

Survival stew—Mmm Mmm Good! Remember all those camping trips you took to practice when you had the luxury of time? How you made the practice into a game for the kids, teaching them how to recognize all the edible plants and insects? And how the crickets continued to escape no matter what type of container you placed them in as you and the kids gathered various plants and insects to add to your evening meal of hardtack, beef jerky, and dried vegetables? Boy did that practice pay off now that you are on the road, walking to your designated safe haven. You know what to gather to supplement your evening hot meal; a hearty soul-warming hot stew of anything found during the day.

How to Dress an Animal

Once you have snared or killed an animal for the stew pot, do you know how to field dress it? There are different types of game, and just about as many different ways to dress it. But since most survivors hardly ever kill a moose or a bear, I will skip the big game part. For our purposes, we will stick to birds, rabbits, and squirrels.

Your first step is to ensure your animal is dead. I can tell you from experience that most small game, while not able to cause serious injury, can scratch or bite you. Use caution and kill the animal before you pick it up. A quick way to dispatch a snared or trapped animal is with a heavy blow to the head with a club, or you can spear it. I prefer to use a club because it kills instantly and the animal does not suffer for long. While I do have to eat, I don't relish the idea of hurting any animal. But as survivors, we must eat, and part of that diet must be animal proteins and fats. Something must die in order for us to live.

Birds—Birds can either be plucked or skinned. I suggest they be plucked. This keeps the skin on the meat, which is full of oils and fats. To pluck them you just need to pull all of the feathers out. For small birds it is easy to do, but with a goose or a turkey, it may take some time. Gut them immediately, keep the inner organs, and cover them with cloth if you have any. This is to keep flies and insects away from them. I recommend in warm weather that your bird be cooked as soon as possible. And, no matter how pretty the picture is of a bird roasting over a fire, make yours into a soup or stew. You should boil it if at all possible because you will need all of the nutrients in the animal. Roasting will allow those important parts of your diet to drip and burn, while boiling retains them.

Rabbits—These are very easy to dress and it only takes a couple of minutes. You can hang the rabbit by its back legs and grasp the skin on a leg. Make a small cut from one ankle down and across to the other ankle. You can now pull the skin down and off, like a glove. Remove the feet and the head. Retain the head for eating. To gut the animal, pinch the upper stomach and make a very small incision. Take the tip of your knife and slowly cut down and then up. That procedure should have opened the stomach cavity. Remove the inner organs, with your hand, using caution not to rupture the bladder (urine). Retain the heart, liver, and kidneys, if they are not spotted. While the thought of it may gross you out, the head and inner organs are very important to your survival diet. You must find a way to cook them that will allow you to eat them. I would suggest you make a stew and just add all of the meats.

Squirrels—Squirrels are a little tougher to skin. It is suggested that you do not hang a squirrel when dressing it. Make a two-inch cross cut about half way down the squirrel's back, grasp the two pieces of skin, and pull them away from each other (pull toward the head and toward the tail). Then, remove the head and feet. Keep the head for cooking. Gut and retain the inner organs just like you did the rabbit. Remember to avoid breaking the bladder or you will get urine on the meat. And when it comes to preparing rodents, you will skin them in the same manner.

The thought of killing, field dressing, and preparing meat is disturbing to some folks, which is easily understood. Nonetheless, in a survival situation, you must learn to prepare your own foods. I have eaten many rabbits, squirrels, rattlesnakes, raccoons, and opossums. In my travels through other countries, I have even eaten monkey, boa (snake), cobra, lizards, and other small animals. You can do the same. You must keep the will to survive alive in your head and you too can make it. Learn to live!

> **Word of caution**—While camping today when you have the time to practice, practice safety so it becomes a natural habit—especially when it comes to food storage. In bear country, we are reminded every day by public campsite warnings to store our food in a secure place: trunk of car, in a bear box usually made of strong metal and locked, or hung by a rope at least 15 feet off the ground. During your walkout to your safe haven, you will need to do the same thing. You must take the time to safeguard your food from animals by hanging it at least 15 feet off the

ground and at least 100 yards from your sleeping area. That will keep the wild animals away.

This brings up another point we need to take into account: when we were forced to walkout to our safe haven, we were part of the millions of other people doing the same thing. In that process, millions of pets were abandoned. And to survive, those pets that were once domestic animals, turned wild. Because of that, you must teach your children to be cautious around what appears to be domestic animals in the wild. Those types of animals are the most dangerous because they have no fear of humans and will be drawn into your camp by the smell of cooked food. Therefore, take precaution. An example, as mentioned in an earlier chapter, is the need for two fires with the fire for cooking food that is separate from the sleeping area. Another step is to clean up after each meal by washing all the plates and cooking utensils. Clean up around the cooking fire to remove all food that has fallen on the ground during the meal and bury all scraps well away from camp. Last but not least, always remember: hungry animals are dangerous animals and they look upon you and your loved ones as food.

Now is the time for you to do the research. Experiment with all the things mentioned in this book. For the sake of your loved ones, become familiar with what is edible and what is not. And please do not make a similar mistake an old friend of mine did when he assumed chocolate milk came from brown cows. Use your God-given common sense and know that the difference between an assumption and the truth could define the fine line between life and death for you and your loved ones.

Weapons, Traps, and Snares

For some people, the idea of being in the wild without a weapon is very scary. In fact, folks often ask, "How do I defend myself?" In a normal camping situation, there is no need for a weapon unless it is being used to assist in procuring food or in camp chores. In most of North America, the need to have a weapon for protection against wild animals is not very great; a survival knife or machete is all that is needed. On the other hand, during your walkout to your safe haven, protection will be a must.

The Need for a Weapon

So you feel the need for a weapon? I agree it is a good idea to have one, but mainly for protection and to kill animals caught in snares, traps, or cornered. If you feel the need for safety and security, and desire to have a large weapon, you can buy one or make one. Make this decision a part of your walkout plan, because many different situations can occur during your walkout to your safe haven. Weapons can be lost, broken, or stolen, leaving you in a survival situation where your loved ones' lives may depend on you knowing how to make replacements. Be prepared because many of the weapons you make will depend on how and where you ended up in your survival situation.

What Kind of Weapon do You Buy?

I know some of you will chuckle at this subtitle for you already know what kind of weapon you'll buy: the biggest you can handle—right? But before you rush down to the local gun dealer, stop for a minute and think about it as a survivalist would.

Gun—If you do not already have a gun, keep in mind that as public tension rises, the government will begin confiscating weapons. If your walkout route takes you through a checkpoint, you may very well find yourself surrendering your weapons to an impatient sergeant as one of his squad members trains an M-16 on you.

Given the erosion of liberties through the Patriot Act, and recently with the implementation of our Homeland Security Act and other similar laws throughout the world, it's not a far reach for government officials to place bans on guns. In the early stages, simpler weapons like bolt action hunting rifles, shotguns, and revolvers, will probably be exempt, but that will likely change in subtle increments. Another thing that will eventually render all of them useless will be the ever-decreasing availability of ammunition.

Hammer—Early man carried a stick with a rock attached to one end. In medieval times in Europe, man exchanged the rock for a piece of metal. When we talk about hammers today, most of us think of those cheap little nail hammers we buy in the discount stores to fix steps and to hang paintings. Hammers like these are completely useless during a walkout, so leave them in your toolbox.

Nonetheless, the great thing about hammer designs of today, is that certain designs make excellent weapons, and there are no laws in the books against carrying a hammer.

With that in mind, what you want is a geologist rock pick/hammer or an oversized claw hammer, known in the construction trade as a roofing hammer or framing hammer. The best place to pick out a good survival hammer is to visit your local sporting goods store, hardware store, or lumberyard. For comparison purposes, start with a top-end model such as a medium weight rock hammer or a 22 to 24 ounce rip claw framing hammer. Heft it for feel. As you do, imagine yourself in the following situations where you are:

- striking an animal that is attacking one of your children;
- defending yourself against a knife-wielding thief;
- clearing low hanging tree limbs and/or digging a fire pit;
- prying loose siding from a collapsed house to make a shelter; or
- using the hammer to claw your way up an embankment.

Then ignore all the price tags and look for a one-piece design; a doubleforged steel head and handle. This design is stronger than a wood or fiberglass handle and more balanced. Make sure the claw hammer has a checkered face design. This type of design helps to keep the hammerhead from slipping off the nail head. The same holds true for anything else. Another great feature of this type of hammer is the slightly curved claw (the straighter the better), whereas a typical home nail hammer has a steeply curved claw.

Do not waist your time purchasing hammers with steeply curved or deeply wedged claws; they were designed for easier nail pulling. The major drawback to this type of design is a weaker tool for digging, clawing and cleaving. Look for a thicker claw design with a shallower wedge. And the last thing you need to look for in the claw hammer is a broad flat handle between the head and the grip with a thin leading edge. This kind of handle will deliver a much more powerful blow than a rounder wood or fiberglass handle. After you have purchased it, if the handle does not have a hole in the end, drill one so you can attach a strong lanyard or wrist strap. The material you use needs to be strong enough to hold your weight while climbing, for battle so you can extend your reach, and to prevent you from dropping it or losing it.

If you choose to buy such a hammer, you will also need a good utility web belt with a hammer holster that you can wear on either hip. The best placement is where you can quickly draw your hammer and swing your backpack off your shoulders to use as a makeshift shield.

When facing a knife-wielding opponent, a hammer like this takes you off the "easy mark" list real fast. This is because your opponent will have to thrust a 4- to 8-inch knife past your backpack shield while you have three times the reach with your hammer. All you need is one good blow anywhere on your attacker's body to deliver a paralyzing, bone-crushing, painful wound. To be able to do that without endangering yourself, practice fighting with your hammer and backpack shield, and stay proficient.

Bow and arrow—There are so many different styles, makes, and models on the market today, this decision will be a personal choice based on what you want to use it for. Think about this and remember it will be easier to make fire-hardened wooden arrows than find needed ammunition for your gun. At the same time, keep in mind that you are packing your survival backpack ounce-by-ounce.

Crossbow—Again there are numerous styles, makes, and models, ranging from small pistol grip crossbows to heavy-duty tri-pod versions. When you are looking at this, also take into consideration your teenage children; this would be a great hunting weapon for the kids.

Blow gun—This weapon comes in many lengths and inner diameters. It is great for hunting small animals on the ground and in the trees.

Slingshot—Whether made of wood or the mighty aluminum wrist-rocket, a slingshot can be as deadly as a twenty-two rifle. Plus there is plenty of ammunition lying on the ground.

When it comes to buying or making a weapon (discussed in the next section), use the example from the movie "Thunder Dome," where Mel Gibson is required to surrender all of his weapons after taking what seems to be five minutes to empty his pockets of more than twenty different kinds. There is no perfect weapon for all situations. Think ahead, plan, and then decide which weapons will be needed for your walkout.

How to Make Weapons

You planned ahead, bought what you needed, and then the worst happens: your weapons were lost, broken, or stolen. What do you do now?

You may have more materials to work with than you think. What about abandoned cars, airplanes, and boats? The weapons you can make from wreckage or a stranded vehicle will be limited only by your imagination. Without any wreckage, the task of making weapons is harder, but not all that difficult.

Take heart and relax; almost anything around you can become a weapon. Those of you who have attended self-defense classes know that a pencil, car key, bottle, book, comb, or even a thumb can become an effective weapons. Regardless of the type of weapon you may want, remember, your imagination will be your only limitation to making the weapons you need. Stop, take a breath and look around you. In some areas you may not have many stones, rocks, or even wood (arctic conditions north of the tree line). In other survival situations you may not even be on land, you may be surrounded by water, or even at sea. In all cases, look around and take inventory of all of your equipment. I have known survivors to use the sharp edges from a ration can to make a crude knife to gut fish with. I have known others who used a sharpened belt buckle to cut with, and still others who field dressed small game with their teeth. You have weapons all around you, so look for them. Keep your imagination active at all times.

Club—One of the most handy survival weapons is a simple club. It is very useful in killing small game and for general camp use. It is simple to make and can be constructed out of many different materials. Using a forked piece of green limb (hard wood works the best), a large rock or piece of bone, and some vine, wire, or rope (remember the parachute cord in your survival pack?), you can make a club in no time.

Make sure the limb has a "Y" section on it and fit the rock into this section, then secure the stone or bone in place using wire, rope, cord, vine, or wet strips of rawhide. Wet strips of rawhide are the best because they will shrink as they dry and hold the stone securely in place.

Knife—A simple knife for stabbing can be made from pieces of bone, antler or a sharp tipped piece of wood. Just break off or locate a piece that is large enough to hold securely and has a sharp point. While you will not be able to cut with it, it is an excellent weapon to stab with.

If you need a knife to cut with, consider using sharp edged bones, chipped edge stone, metal from wreckage, wood, or even glass for the blade. In a survival situation, you may have to use what you can find to make tools and weapons with. Almost any sharp edge from any hard material can be used. If you want to take the time to make an effective knife, find a piece of green hard wood, split it slightly, insert your blade, and then wrap the handle tightly. Once again, wet strips of rawhide makes the best wrap because they shrink when they dry and will hold the blade firmly in place.

Spear—Another weapon that is easy to make is a spear. It is very useful in killing any game you don't want to touch or get too close to. An example might be a snake, porcupine, skunk, or animals with horns, antlers, teeth, fangs, and hooves; they can all cause unnecessary injuries to you or your family. A spear can be made as simply as sharpening the end of long, green piece of wood and hardening it in a fire. Or, you can attach a blade point using the same types of materials you used for your knife blade. And, the spear point can be attached exactly like your knife blade was, using wire, vine, string, cord, or wet strips of rawhide. An easier way to attach a point to a spear shaft is to simply tie it on. Place a knife parallel to and tightly up against the shaft of the spear. Then latch it on securely.

Slingshot—For the slingshot, you start by cutting a Y-shaped piece of green wood, cutting two strips of rubber (from a tire or rubber tubing) about eight inches long, and making a pouch from either cloth or leather. Secure the two strips of rubber on both sides of the Y on the wood near the top, tie the pouch to the open ends of the rubber strips, and you now have a weapon. You can use small pebbles as ammunition. I assure you with practice you can procure a bird or rabbit for dinner. A hint here: use two or three small pebbles when you shoot—makes it more likely to hit a target.

Bola—The bola is much more difficult to use but is simple to make. Tie all three ends of the pieces of string or parachute cord together at one end. At the other ends, tie a stone on each piece of line. You now have three cords with a stone on each end that meets and is secured at the other end. To use the bola, grasp the tied end, twirl it over your head, and release it toward your target. Once you release the bola, it opens up and covers a very wide path. While it is very effective against birds, it can also wrap around the legs of larger game and trip it. Then, using your newly made spear and knife, you can kill it and process the meat.

There will be unlimited resources on your walkout that can be used as weapons. Keep in mind that some of the materials useful to make weapons may not be recognized as such by most people. Bone, glass, rough metals, stones, antlers, horns, and other materials can be modified for use as weapons. Keep your survival mind active and evaluate all material at hand. While the making and using of primitive weapons takes some time, it can be done. I suggest using your spear to stab with, not throw. If you only have one spear and you throw it, what do you do if the animal turns on you? Remember, do not throw the only weapon you have available—keep it in your hands. Plus, depending on the type of blade you have used on your spear, you may break it.

Another thing to keep in mind, the weapons that have been discussed were used by early man many years ago and they were deadly in the hands of a person who knew how to use them. The Native Americans kept their families alive with such weapons by providing both food and protection. If others can do it, so can you. Therefore, take the time you have now, and have fun experimenting.

Snares and Traps

When it comes to procuring meat in the wild, you will have to work for your next meal. Usually, it takes a lot of work. Animals are difficult for the inexperienced hunter to catch. They are very shy of man and often their senses are highly tuned toward survival. However, you can trap most small game with patience, patience, and more patience.

There are all kinds of traps that can be made in the bush. Some use boulders, huge logs, deep pits, and so on. Those are more work than they are worth. Well, at least they are for the average person who needs meat quickly and is not hunting large game. To keep this process as simple as possible for your walkout survival plan, we will concentrate on small game. Mainly because they are easier to trap and they are more abundant. Not to mention, they are less dangerous to catch.

The best plan of action on a walkout is to always be alert to small animals as you travel to your safe haven and shoot them with one of your weapons. Then in the evening, once you have decided on a campsite, use snares with the hope of catching a meal for the next day.

Snares—can be purchased ready made, with a locking loop. Or, if you prefer, you can make your own from wire, string, cord or vines. I have found wire to work the best and as you may have guessed, vines work less effectively. But, in a survival situation, if you don't have an item with you, then you must use what Mother Nature provides.

I can tell you from experience, it will take a lot of traps to yield one animal, unless you get lucky and discover a place that is full of small game! I recommend you set them out by the dozens and check them first thing each morning. Try to find small game trails, which are small trails through the grass and weeds. Often, rabbits and other small game use the same trails over and over as they travel to food and water sources. Like man, they are creatures of habit. You may also find trails that lead into briar patches, thorn bushes, and other types of brush. Small game use these as places of protection or places to hide. They are good places to put a snare as well.

When making a snare there are two very common designs. One type of design simply holds the animal at ground level and may or may not strangle the victim. The second design will flip the animal into the air, strangling it as the trap holds the carcass off of the ground.

Both designs require the loop in the wire, cord, string, or vine, to tighten and hold the animal. The loop should be free moving. This free movement allows the loop to tighten as the animal struggles or moves forward into the snare. With the flip-up design, movement of the wire will trigger the device and fling the animal into the air, which, using the animal's body weight, tightens the loop. Make sure the loop has free movement.

Holding snare—For the holding snare (see Figure 10-1), let's say for a rabbit, you make a loop about four inches in diameter and place it about two inches above the center of the game trail. For a squirrel, you make a loop about three inches in diameter and two to three inches above the trail. Make sure the end of the snare wire, opposite the loop, is secured to a bush, stake, or other stationary object. Make sure what you use to secure the snare cannot be pulled away by the animal. Then, if needed, use brush, logs or other debris to make a funnel toward your snare. In other words, force the animal to the snare and do not allow them to go around it. Since most animals will continue to use a trail they have used daily, this should not be a big issue. By using the tunneling effect, the game will usually continue down the known trail. The animal's head will then enter the loop and as it continues to move forward the loop will slide and become smaller. Eventually the loop will be so small in size the animal cannot get out. Any struggling will only tighten the loop. Thus, you have dinner.

Flip-up snare—This principle is the same as far as tunneling the animal. The difference is when the animal's head enters the snare it will pull the wire far enough to trigger the flip-up or trip part of the trap. At that point, the animal will be flipped into the air and strangled. The diameter of the loop and the distances off the ground remain the same in this snare as in the other.

To make a trip snare, you need a flexible limb or bush, the snare wire, a trigger and a method to hold the trigger. The easiest trigger mechanism is displayed in the diagram. (See Figure 10-1.) Test the trigger to ensure it slips off with the slightest tug. I do not recommend this type of snare in extreme cold because the flexible part of the trap often freezes in place and does not function as a spring any longer. If the weather is really cold use the standard holding snare.

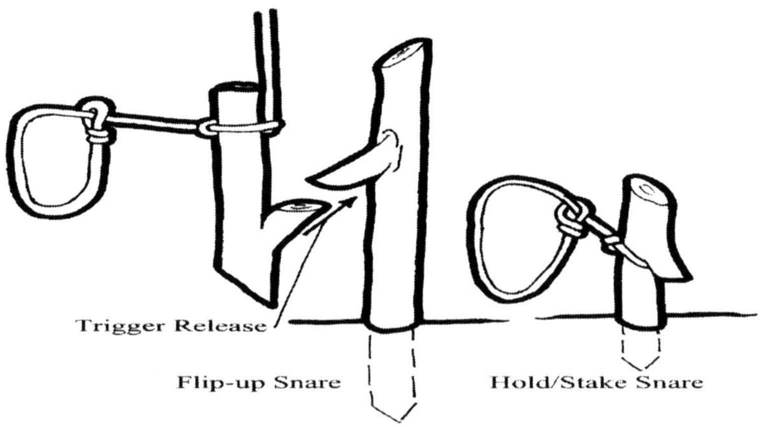

Figure 10 - 1 Two Types of Snares

I stated earlier in this article to check your traps each morning. This is important to remember. Some animals, if snared by the leg, will actually chew their leg off to get out of the trap. And until you arrive to retrieve your catch, it can become a meal for any passerby—animal or human.

Traps—Earlier in the book I recommended you carry large rattraps to use in your efforts to catch your supper. No matter what type of trap you eventually decide to use, all traps, including snares, need to be placed in the game trail. *Always* anchor them down.

Seesaw trap—Very similar to the flip-up snare, this is a good trap for the beginner because it is easy to balance properly. (See Figure 10-2.) This trap can be used on a game trail, or you can also use bait placed in front of the loop. The idea is when the animal takes the bait, the limb moves, the weight falls, and the animal is flipped into the air. This trap may or may not kill the animal, but the weight will keep small game from running away. Again, remember to anchor it.

Figure 10 - 2 Seesaw Trap

Fish trap—The easiest way to trap fish is to build a funnel between two objects to guide fish into shallow water and then make something to block the funnel to prevent the fish from escaping when you try to catch them. Now you are ready to go downstream and drive the fish toward the funnel.

Catching Tools

A simple tool to catch wild animals, if cornered, is using a loop of wire, like that used with a snare, tied to a long stick or limb. Remember, even small animals like rabbits, raccoons, or others can scratch and even bite. Keep in mind: after you capture the animal, you will have to kill it.

Another tool to help catch fish is your hands. To my amazement, I was instructed to wade out into the water, stand with my feet spread apart a little wider than my shoulders and then bend over and place my hands in the water with my palms facing up, with my fingertips of one hand barely touching the finger tips of the other hand. After standing there for about five minutes, a small rainbow trout swam into my hands and I was able to throw it ashore. I'd seen this done on TV, but never believed it until I was able to do it myself. This method of catching fish does work and it will place food on the table when you've lost your fishing kit.

Doing What It Takes to Survive

For some of you, snaring an animal may not be a very pleasant task. It may prove to be even more difficult to kill an animal so you can eat. Survival is not a game. In a real survival situation, your life and the lives of your loved ones may very well depend on your ability to snare game, eat insects, or even the consumption of certain plants you may not like. It is necessary for the success of your walkout plan. This brings up a question: Can you adapt and do what it takes for you and your family to survive? Yes, you can!

A Safe Walkout

In the unpredictable world of survival, you need to be prepared for the unexpected. Because something like this could happen to you:

> It was a gorgeous mid-summer day, warm but not to warm. I was enjoying the afternoon and the company of an old friend as we hiked up a switchback trail that I had traveled many times over the last few years. As we talked, I was also keeping an eye out for a lookout point along the trail, an opening in the trees that gave us a spectacular view of the valley below. As we approached the opening, I turned my head to look back at my friend, stepped on a patch of rock-shale, slipped, and extended my knee, causing a very painful injury. After taking a break and looking at my injury, we decided to head back down the switchbacks to a meadow about a mile away. At the bottom of the switchback, the trail crossed a small creek of cool water and I decided to use it to try and bring down the swelling in my knee. Resting, and soaking my knee in the water helped me recoup. But before I safely finished crossing the creek, I slipped and fell, soaking myself to the chest. Even though the meadow we wanted to reach was only about a hundred yards away, I was soaked, my knee hurt again due to the fall, and the wind had come up. By the time we reached the meadow, my knee was badly swollen, I was wet, in pain, chilled to the bone, and the temperature was dropping as the sun set behind the mountains. Luckily, my friend helped me with my pack, wrapped me in a blanket, started a fire near me, and set up camp. The next morning my knee was much better and we had a safe hike back to the vehicle.

No matter how prepared you may think you are, the weather, the terrain, and other people also trying to survive will be unknown factors. Be prepared!

Dress for the Unexpected

Even in areas of mild weather, the temperature can change dramatically as the time of day changes. Deserts that are hot during the day can be cold at night. Sudden rain showers can change a mild day into a cold one. Climbing steep mountains can cause a person to sweat, making his cloths wet, making him feel cold in the wind.

The point is, dress in layers so you can remove clothing and put it in your pack as the temperature warms up or as you exert yourself. As the temperature drops, or you slow your pace, you can put the layers back on.

Most important, don't go off without a hat. During cool or cold weather, as much as 75 percent of your body heat loss can be through your uncovered head. This can be critical during a period of survival, especially during the night when you are trying to rest.

Wear clothing to match the climate. Don't push your luck in bad weather. A day spent in camp during a dense fog, snowstorm, or thunderstorm, is much better than a night in a survival camp dealing with hypothermia and wishing you were dry and warm.

Crossing Water

Another danger is crossing bodies of water, whether they be lakes, rivers, creeks, or flooded areas. When we come upon river rapids, we know the condition of that water. The problem arises when we approach what initially appears to be calm water or still, muddy water. The surface looks calm, but what is the water like closer to the bottom? Is it shallow? Or is it deep? And how deep is it?

The first thing to do is look for fallen trees or obstacles that cross the water. If none are available, but there are fallen trees in the area and enough people in your group, you can construct a bridge by placing two tree trunks side-by-side spanning the water. By using two tree trunks you have minimized the danger of slipping, falling in, or being injured in the process.

This situation is another example of the importance of having a hiking staff. If you are unable to construct a bridge and need to walk across the water, use the hiking staff to probe the water ahead of you. Make sure you create ample activity in the process to scare away any unseen water predators that may be lying in wait.

Is a Bridge Safe?

Seeking out and crossing bridges sounds like the easiest thing to do Maybe. And maybe not! Remember, you will be a small group of a populace of several million people seeking safety. Among those other people will be groups of individuals who see an opportunity to rob unsuspecting travelers of their goods. Bridges, narrow gaps along roadways, and canyons, are prime areas to set up checkpoints and to spring an ambush. Bandits, pirates, and marauders will be out there waiting for any chance to better themselves at your cost. Be careful. Be vigilant. Be safe.

Bad People Doing Bad Things

During my time in the military and afterwards as a counselor and consultant, I have witnessed examples of the horrific atrocities humans are capable of inflicting on fellow humans. I have seen good people change under stressful situations, whether it is in time of war, during combat, in a disaster, after an accident, or even while having an argument. I have watched good people mentally crack and some never made it back. Good people, like the ones I knew will be out there trying to cope with life after a nation-wide catastrophe, will do things never thought of during their present day-to-day life.

And there is another group of people. This group is made up of immature adults whose personal fears of spending time in jail basically keep them from becoming more than a bully or thug. I have watched these people enter a safe and secure campground and harass the campers, and then tell the police officers that they were just having fun and meant no harm. My concern is: What will these people be like in the lawless aftermath of a nation-wide catastrophe? How will they affect you? What will you do when they enter your camp? How will you protect your wife and daughter? Will you try to accommodate them with the hopes they will go away? Will you submit and possibly become their slaves? Or will you (as I explained in an earlier chapter) become mad-dog-mean, hit harder that they do, hit faster than they do and then melt away? You and your loved ones may have to face and survive a similar situation during your walkout. What will you do?

Dealing with Winter Terrain

One of the most difficult survival situations is a cold weather scenario. Remember, cold weather by itself is a very dangerous adversity. Every time you venture into the cold, you are pitting yourself and your loved ones against the elements. And winter weather is highly variable. Prepare yourself to adapt to blizzard conditions even during sunny and clear weather.

Dealing with Cold Weather

There are four basic principles to follow to keep warm. An easy way to remember these basic principles is to use the word *COLD*:

C—Keep clothing clean. This principle is always important for sanitation and comfort. In winter, it is also important from the standpoint of warmth. Clothes matted with dirt and grease lose much of their insulation value. Heat can escape more easily from the body through the clothing's crushed or filled air pockets.

O—Avoid overheating. When you get too hot, you sweat and your clothing absorbs the moisture. This affects your warmth in two ways: (1) dampness decreases the insulation quality of clothing, and (2) as sweat evaporates, your body cools. Adjust your clothing so that you do not sweat. Do this by partially opening your coat, jacket, or vest; by removing an inner layer of clothing; by removing gloves; throwing back the hood of your coat; or removing your hat for a few minutes. The head and hands act as efficient heat dissipaters when overheated.

L—Wear your clothing loose and in layers. Wearing tight clothing and foot gear restricts blood circulation and invites cold injury. It also decreases the volume of air trapped between the layers, reducing its insulating value. Several layers of lightweight clothing are better than one equally thick layer of clothing, because the layers have dead-air space between them. The dead-air space provides extra insulation. Also, layers of clothing allow you to take off or add clothing layers to either prevent excessive sweating or to increase warmth.

D—Keep clothing dry. In cold temperatures, your inner layers of clothing can become wet from sweat, and your outer layer, if not water repellent, can become wet from snow and frost melted by body heat. Wear water repellent outer clothing, if available. It will shed most of the water collected from melting snow and frost. Another precaution you can take is to brush off the snow and frost before entering a heated shelter.

Despite the precautions you take, there will be times when you cannot keep from getting wet. At such times, drying your clothing may become a major problem. On the march, hang your damp mittens and socks on your rucksack. Sometimes in freezing temperatures, the wind and sun will dry this clothing. You can also place damp socks or mittens, unfolded, near your body so that your body heat can dry them. In a campsite, hang damp clothing inside the shelter near the top, using drying lines or improvised racks. You may even be able to dry each item by holding it before an open fire. Dry leather items slowly. If no other means are available for drying your boots, put them between your sleeping bag shell and liner. Your body heat will help to dry the leather.

Frostbite—This injury is the result of frozen tissues. Light frostbite involves only the skin that takes on a dull whitish pallor. Deep frostbite extends to a depth below the skin. The tissues become solid and immovable. Your feet, hands, and exposed facial areas are particularly vulnerable to frostbite.

The best frostbite prevention, when you are with others, is to use the buddy system. Check your buddy's face often and make sure that he checks yours. If you are alone, periodically cover your nose and lower part of your face with your gloved hand, with your bandanna, or with a spare item of clothing.

The following pointers will aid you in keeping warm and preventing frostbite when it is extremely cold or when you have less than adequate clothing:

- *Face*—Maintain circulation by twitching and wrinkling the skin on your face. Warm with your hands.
- *Ears*—Wiggle and move your ears. Warm with your hands.
- *Hands*—Move your hands inside your gloves. Warm by placing your hands close to your body.
- *Feet*—Move your feet and wiggle your toes inside your boots.

A loss of feeling in your hands and feet is a sign of frostbite. If you have lost feeling for only a short time, the frostbite is probably light. Otherwise, assume the frostbite is deep. To rewarm a light frostbite, use your hands or gloves to warm your face and ears. Place your hands under your armpits. Place your feet next to your buddy's stomach. A deep frostbite injury, if thawed and refrozen, will cause more damage than a nonmedical trained person can handle. Here is a list of do's and don'ts regarding frostbite.

Do:

- Periodically check for Frostbite.
- Rewarm light frostbite.
- Keep injured areas from refreezing.

Don't:

- Rube injury with snow.
- Drink alcoholic beverage.
- Smoke.
- Try to thaw out a deep frostbite if away from medical assistance.

Note—A deep frostbite is when the skin has turned black. The procedure to thaw this type requires a very slow warming process starting with cold water. Even when done correctly this is a very painful procedure.

Trench foot and immersion foot—These conditions result from many hours or days of exposure to wet or damp conditions at a temperature just above freezing. The symptoms are a sensations of pins and needles, tingling, numbness, and then pain. The skin will initially appear wet, soggy, white, and shriveled. As it progresses and damage appears, the skin will take on a red and then a bluish or black discoloration. The feet become cold, swollen, and have a waxy appearance. Walking becomes difficult and the feet feel heavy and numb. The nerves and muscles sustain the main damage, but gangrene can occur. In extreme cases, the flesh dies and it may become necessary to have the foot or leg amputated. The best prevention is to keep your feet dry. Remember those extra socks you packed away in a waterproof packet? You can also dry wet socks against your torso (back or chest). The best thing to do is wash your feet and put on dry socks daily.

Sunburn—Exposed skin can become sunburned even when the air temperature is below freezing. The sun's rays reflect at all angles from snow, ice, and water, hitting sensitive areas of skin such as lips, nostrils, and eyelids. Exposure to the sun results in sunburn more quickly at high altitudes than at low altitudes. Apply sunburn cream or lip salve to your face when in the sun. The best solution is to cover your face with a bandanna.

Snow blindness—The reflection of the sun's ultraviolet rays off a snow-covered area causes this condition. The symptoms of snow blindness are a sensation of grit in the eyes, pain in and over the eyes that increases with eyeball movement, red and teary eyes, and a headache that intensifies with continued exposure to light. Prolonged exposure to these rays can result in permanent eye damage. To treat snow blindness, bandage your eyes until the symptoms disappear.

You can prevent snow blindness by wearing sunglasses. If you don't have sunglasses, improvise to limit the amount of light to your eyes. Cut slits in a piece of cardboard, thin wood, tree bark, or other available material. (See Figure 11-1.) Also, putting black soot from your fireplace under your eyes will help reduce shine and glare.

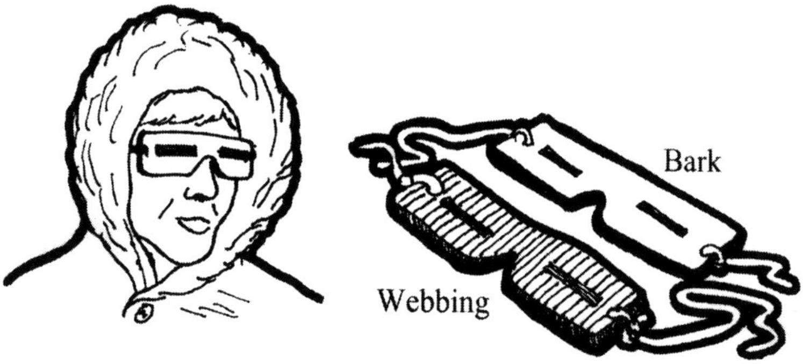

Figure 11 - 1 Snow Sunglasses

Crossing Tropical Terrain

Most people think of the tropics as huge and forbidding tropical rain forests through which every step taken must be hacked out, and where every inch of the way is crawling with danger. Actually, over half of the land in the tropics is cultivated in some way.

To increase the prospect of you and your loved ones passing through this terrain successfully, you must have an understanding of the various types of tropics (including the tropics and tropical swamps of North America), have the ability to improvise, and the will to live by using the principles of survival. Do not be afraid of being alone in the jungle. Fear will lead to panic, and panic will lead to exhaustion and decrease your chances of survival.

Everything in the tropics thrives, including disease, germs, and parasites that breed at an alarming rate. Other than that, nature will provide you will ample water, food, and plenty of materials to build shelters.

Weather—High temperatures, heavy rainfall, and oppressive humidity characterize equatorial and subtropical regions, except at high altitudes. At low altitudes, temperature variation is seldom less than 50 degrees Fahrenheit (10 degrees Celsius) and is often more than 95 degrees Fahrenheit (35 degrees Celsius). At altitudes over 4,500 feet (1,500 meters), ice often forms at night. The rain has a cooling effect, but when it stops, the temperature soars.

Rainfall is heavy, often with thunder and lightning. Sudden rain beats on the tree canopy, turning trickles into raging torrents and causing rivers to rise. Just as suddenly, the rain stops. Violent storms may occur, usually toward the end of the summer months.

Hurricanes, cyclones, and typhoons develop over the sea and rush inland, causing tidal waves and devastation ashore. In choosing campsites, make sure you are above any potential flooding. Prevailing winds vary between winter and summer. The dry season has rain once a day and the monsoon has continuous rain.

Types of Tropical Terrain

There is no standard jungle. The tropical area may be any of the following:

Tropical rain forests—The climate varies little in rain forests. You find these forests across the equator in the Amazon and Congo basins, parts of Indonesia, and several Pacific islands. Up to 5 feet (3.5 meters) of rain falls evenly throughout the year. Temperatures range from about 89 degrees Fahrenheit (32 degrees Celsius) during the day, to 70 degrees Fahrenheit (21 degrees Celsius) at night.

There are five layers of vegetation in this jungle. Where untouched by man, jungle trees rise from buttress roots to heights of 60 meters. Below them, smaller trees produce a canopy so thick that little light reaches the jungle floor. Seedlings struggle beneath them to reach light, and masses of vines and lianas twine up to the sun. Ferns, mosses, and herbaceous plants push through a thick carpet of leaves, and a great variety of fungi grow on leaves and fallen tree trunks. Because of the lack of light on the jungle floor, there is little undergrowth to hamper movement, but dense growth limits visibility to about 50 meters. You can easily lose your sense of direction in this jungle.

Saltwater swamps—Saltwater swamps are common in coastal areas subject to tidal flooding. Mangrove trees thrive in these swamps. Mangrove trees can reach heights of 36 feet (12 meters), and their tangled root system create major obstacles that hamper movement. Visibility in this type of swamp is poor, and movement is extremely difficult. Sometimes, streams that you can raft form channels, but you usually end up traveling on foot through this swamp.

Everything in a saltwater swamp may appear hostile to you, from leeches and insects to crocodiles and caimans. Avoid the dangerous animals in this swamp. Avoid this swamp altogether if you can. If there are water channels through it, use a raft to pass through.

Freshwater swamps—You find freshwater swamps in low-lying inland areas. They contain masses of thorny undergrowth, reeds, grasses, and occasional short palms that reduce visibility and make travel difficult. There are often islands that dot these swamps, allowing you to get out of the water. Wildlife is abundant in these swamps.

Crossing Desert Terrain

There are several things you need to be familiar with for you and your loved ones to survive in arid or desert areas; you must understand and prepare for the environment you will face. You must plan your equipment needs, the procedures you will use, and how the environment will affect you and your initial strategy. Your survival will depend upon your knowledge of the terrain, basic climatic elements, your ability to cope with these elements, and your will to live.

Terrain—Desert terrain makes movement difficult and demanding. Land navigation will be extremely difficult as there may be very few landmarks. Cover- and shelter- making material may be very limited; therefore, the problem of exposure to the elements and to other groups of travelers remains constant.

- *Mountain deserts*—Mountain deserts are characterized by scattered ranges or areas of barren hills or mountains separated by dry, flat basins. High ground may rise gradually or abruptly from flat areas to 12,000 feet (4000 meters) above sea level. Most of the infrequent rainfall occurs on high ground and runs off rapidly in the form of flash floods. These floodwaters erode deep gullies and ravines and deposit sand and gravel around the edges of the basins. Water rapidly evaporates, leaving the land as barren as before, although there may be short-lived vegetation. If enough water enters the basin to compensate for the rate of evaporation, shallow lakes may develop, such as the Great Salt Lake in Utah, or the Dead Sea. Most of these lakes have a high salt content.
- *Rocky plateau deserts*—Rocky plateau deserts have relatively slight relief interspersed with extensive flat areas with quantities of solid or broken rock at or near the surface. There may be steep-walled,

eroded valleys, known as arroyos or canyons in the United States and Mexico. Although their flat bottoms may be superficially attractive as assembly areas, the narrower valleys can be extremely dangerous to you and your loved ones due to flash flooding after rain storms, even from floods that happen several miles away.

- *Sandy or dune deserts*—Sandy or dune deserts are extensive flat areas covered with sand or gravel. "Flat" is a relative term, as some areas may contain sand dunes that are over 900 feet (300 meters) high and 10 to 15 miles (16 to 24 kilometers) long. To travel in such terrain will depend on the windward or leeward slope of the dunes and the texture of the sand. Other areas, however, may be flat for 9,000 feet (3,000 meters) and more. Plant life may vary from none to scrub over 6 feet (2 meters) high. This type of desert area is found in California, Oklahoma, and New Mexico.
- *Salt marshes*—Salt marshes are flat, desolate areas, sometimes studded with clumps of grass but devoid of other vegetation. They occur in arid areas where rainwater has collected, evaporated, and left large deposits of alkali salts, and water with a high salt concentration. The water is so salty it is undrinkable. A crust that may be 1–12 inches (2.5 to 30 centimeters) thick, forms over the saltwater.

  In arid areas there are salt marshes encompassing hundreds of kilometers. These areas usually support many insects, most of which bite. Avoid salt marshes. This type of terrain is highly corrosive to boots, clothing, and skin.
- *Broken terrain*—All arid areas contain broken or highly dissected terrain. Rainstorms that erode soft sand and carve out canyons form this terrain. An arroyo may range from 9 feet (3 meters) wide and 6 feet (2 meters) deep to several hundred meters wide and deep. The direction it takes varies as much as its width and depth. It twists and turns and forms a maze-like pattern. An arroyo will give you good cover and concealment, but do not try to move through it because it is very difficult terrain to negotiate.

Heat Problems

The chances of you or one of your loved ones becoming a heat casualty as you traverse this terrain are great. This danger increases with injury, stress, and the loss or lack of critical survival items. The following are the major types of heat casualties and their treatment when little water and no medical help are available.

Heat cramps—The loss of salt due to excessive sweating causes heat cramps. Symptoms range from moderate to severe muscle cramps in legs, arms, or abdomen. These symptoms may start as a mild muscular discomfort. At this point, you should now stop all activity, get in the shade, and drink water. If you fail to recognize the early symptoms and continue walking, you will have severe muscle cramps and pain. Treat the same as heat exhaustion, below.

Heat exhaustion—A large loss of body water and salt causes heat exhaustion. Symptoms include headache, mental confusion, irritability, excessive sweating, weakness, dizziness, cramps, and pale, moist, and cold (clammy) skin. Immediately get the patient in the shade. Make him lie on a stretcher or similar item about 1.5 feet (45 centimeters) off the ground. Loosen his clothing. Sprinkle him with water and fan him. Have him drink small amounts of water every 3 minutes. Ensure he stays quiet and rests. If he should go into convulsions, try to keep him from hurting himself; if possible, place a small bite stick or wallet between his teeth to prevent him from biting his tongue. Then patiently wait for the convulsions to pass. Then continue the process of cooling him down.

Heat stroke—A severe heat injury caused by extreme loss of water and salt and the body's inability to cool itself. The patient may die if not cooled immediately. Symptoms include the lack of sweat, hot and dry skin, headache, dizziness, fast pulse, nausea and vomiting, and mental confusion leading to unconsciousness. Immediately get the person to some shade. Lay him on a stretcher or similar item about 1.5 feet (45 centimeters) off the ground. Loosen his clothing. Pour water on him (it does not matter if the water is polluted or brackish) and fan him. Massage his arms, legs, and body. If he regains consciousness, let him drink small amounts of water every 3 minutes.

Desert Hazards

There are several hazards unique to desert survival. These include snakes, thorny plants and cacti, contaminated water, sunburn, eye irritation, climatic stress, and last but not least, insects.

Dealing with Insects

You will have to deal with insects of almost every type in all terrain and in all types of weather conditions. The main problem with insects is that you and your loved ones are a source of water and food for lice, mites, wasps, flies, mosquitoes, and various other insects. As you walk to your safe haven, remember: old buildings, ruins, and caves are favorite habitats of spiders, scorpions, centipedes, lice, and mites. These areas provide protection from the elements and also attract other wildlife. Therefore, take extra care when staying in these areas. Wear gloves at all times. Do not place your hands anywhere without first looking to see what is there. Visually inspect an area before sitting or lying down. When you get up, shake everything out, inspect the clothing you have on, your boots, and other clothing articles before putting them on.

All areas have snakes. They inhabit ruins, garbage dumps, caves, and natural rock outcropping that offer shade. Never go barefoot or walk through these areas without carefully inspecting them for snakes. Pay attention to where you place your feet and hands. Most snakebites result from stepping on or handling snakes. Avoid them. Once you see a snake, give it a wide berth.

Few things can ruin your day more than hordes of mosquitoes or black flies. In large numbers, they can be very dangerous. Even in cold areas, a sudden warm snap can bring the pests out in large numbers.

In bug country, you should always wear a long-sleeved shirt and trousers. Apply a repellent to the clothing as well as any exposed skin.

In your preparation for evening camp, pick a site with insect control in mind. Stay away from pools of stagnant water or dead things. Pick sites where you can take advantage of any breeze that may help keep the insects away.

When there is no repellent, the first thing to do is cover up all exposed skin area. Tuck trouser legs into boots. Button sleeves tight around the wrists. Pull up shirt and coat collars to protect the neck. Put on a hat and gloves. In short, give the biting critters as small a target as possible.

Next, if possible and safe to do so, build a smoky fire near your shelter—the smokier the better. But remember, it will run off the insects and you, and it will also tell people miles away where you are.

Do not forget there are pests other than the flying type.

While ticks are a potential long-term health threat with disease such as Lyme disease or Rocky Mountain spotted fever, they do not pose the immediate threat that the larger numbers of flying pests do. Ticks should be avoided, and when found on the body, removed.

The recommended way to remove an embedded tick is to use tweezers and gently but firmly pull the tick straight out. Avoid jerking or twisting the tick, as the head may remain embedded. Do not burn them first. The tick's boiling guts will be injected into the wound. After removing the tick, wash the bite area with soap and water and apply an antiseptic if you can.

Regular Bowel Movements and Personal Hygiene

Last but not least, is the need to ensure everyone in your party continues to have regular bowel movements, especially the children. And again the best cure for constipation is the white ash from your campfire. For diarrhea, use small amount of the black ash from the campfire. Ensure everyone is drinking a quart (32 ounces) to two quarts of water a day.

Personal hygiene is also a must to ensure the safe arrival of your family at the safe haven. An innocent scratch left unattended can cause infections and even lead to death. Your first priority is to take care of your family. You do not want people becoming sick, ill, or worse when you are running for your lives. Take care and be safe.

If You Are in Trouble—STOP

Your most important survival skill is your ability to admit that you are lost. That is not an easy decision to make. Most people will not admit that until they have wandered around for long periods getting into a worse situation than they would have been in had they recognized their predicament at the beginning.

Once you admit that you are lost, sit down and think. Get control of yourself, avoid panic, and stay calm. Mentally, you must accept the challenge you are facing and make the best of the adventure. Remember, you are not alone; your family is with you and you do not want to add additional stress to an already stressful situation.

Let's face it, avoiding panic is difficult when dealing with yourself, your spouse, and your children. It was up to you to lead your family to the safe haven and now you're lost. Most people who get lost panic to some degree but those who fare best are those who get control of their thoughts quickly. In extreme cases, those who panic may forget who they are or where they are. You have a choice. Get a grip.

The first thing to do when you admit to yourself that you are lost is to resist the temptation to walk or run your way out of the situation. STOP! Rest and remember: STOP.

S—Sit. The act of sitting down will help keep you from getting into deeper trouble. This one act alone can jump-start the thinking process, and it helps suppress the urge to run or make hasty, foolish decisions.

T—Think survival. Each day will be a challenge to stay alive. Your mind is the best survival tool you have. In such a situation, you are at the mercy of your mind. In order to survive, you must keep control by thinking of past training, experiences, and by maintaining a positive mental attitude. Develop the determination to survive. Think of your goal: to help your family reach the safe haven.

O—Observe your surroundings to discover what problems must be resolved and what resources you have to solve them with. You need shelter, fire, water and a campsite. Get the family involved, make job assignments. Get everyone involved. Keep everyone busy. Keep everyone positive.

P—Plan ahead. Now that you are settled down and ready to live the adventure, adjust your plans and set them into motion.

Get comfortable, enjoy the unexpected and unique experience, and get ready for the next day by having a warm, good night's sleep. And when you wake, you will be facing a new day.

The tragedy of any disaster is that parents will endure the hardships only to see their children perish along the way, and when the earth begins to heal, they will be barren. During the same time, there will also be children who have watched their own parents meet a similar fate. In the loneliest of times, have faith—for life will help the children and the barren parents find each other, and there will be love, and there will be family. Life will continue!

Annotated Bibliography

A

American Institute of Aeronautics and Astronautics (AIAA)—www.aiaa.com
    Space Weather
American Physical Society—prola.aps.org
    Comets
    Cosmic-Ray Intensity
    Geomagnetic Storms
    Radiation Intensity—Time variations
    Solar Flares
    Solar Storms
    UV Theory

B

Boy Scouts of America Handbook

D

Department of Health—www.hhs.gov
    Disasters and Emergencies
    Safety and Wellness
Department Homeland Security—www.dhs.gov
    Prevention and Protection
    Preparedness and Response

F

Federal Emergency Management Agency (FEMA)—www.fema.gov
    Types of Disasters

I

Institute of Medicine—www.iom.edu
Disaster response (workshop summaries)

K

Kolbrin, The - edited by the Culdian Trust—www.thekolbrin.com

M

Medieval Weapons—www.historicalweapons.com
Axes
Bows
Crossbows
Hammers
Slings
Spears

N

National Aeronautics and Space Administration (NASA)- www.nasa.gov
Solar Storms, make up and effects
National Library of Medicine—www.nlm.nih.gov
All health issues discussed in this book
National Oceanic and Atmosphere Administration (NOAA)—www.noaa.gov
National Weather Administration
Weather Safety
Storm Ready
Tsunami Ready
New York Times/Health—www.nytimes.com/health
Various articles on health and survival

P

Post-Traumatic Stress Disorders edited by Tom Williams, Psy.D.
Psychiatric Dictionary by Robert J. Campbell

T

Theory and Practice of Group Psychotherapy by Irvin D. Yalom

U

U.S. Air Force Survival Guide
U.S. Army Ranger Digest
U.S. Army Survival Manual
U.S. Department of Defense

U.S. Geological Service (USGS)—www.usgs.gov
Climate Change
Earthquakes
Floods
Human Health
Volcanoes
Water Quality
Wild Fires
U.S. Navy S.E.R.E. Training Manual
U.S. Navy Survival Guide

W

WebMD—www.webmd.com
All health issues discussed in this book
Wikipedia, the Free Encyclopedia—www.en.wikipedia.org
Agricultural Science
Asteroids
Barter (system, economics & Finance)
Coronal Mass Ejections (CME)
Geomagnetic Storms
Meteors
Solar Flares
Solar Storms
Sunspots
Survival
Survival Skills
Survival kits
Survivalism (survival after social upheaval)
Weapons
World Bank—www.worldbank.org
Economic Projections—econ.worldbank.org and sitesources.worldbank.org

Index

S

T

U

V

W

X

About the Author

Dr. Brent Lee is a graduate of the United States Navy S.E.R.E. (Survival, Evasion, Resistance and Escape) School. He also attended several military and civilian survival schools in California, Guam, and the Philippines. Lee also served one tour as a Combat Search and Rescue Aircrewman in Vietnam, and during another tour in the Pacific, he was a member of the Search and Rescue Response Team in Guam. Lee has survived numerous disasters. Since his retirement from the United States Navy in 1993, he has kept his survival skills honed through exploring the wondrous Rocky Mountains near his home in Wyoming.

Additionally, Lee is a Consultant in Alternative Ways, and author of the nonfiction, *Beyond Knowing*; and the fiction, *Epicenter*. Lee holds a PhD in Philosophy, a MA in Counseling Psychology, and a BA in Theology. As a consultant, he specializes in personal, professional, and spiritual guidance through regressive and meditative therapy. Lee's philosophy is, "Man is made by his belief. As he believes, so he is."

Lee wishes to thank you for taking the time to read this book and extends an invitation to you to visit with him through his website at: www.brentlee.com.

0 26575 52231 0